With Respect to Readers_____

DIMENSIONS OF LITERARY RESPONSE

With Respect to Readers

DIMENSIONS OF LITERARY RESPONSE

WALTER J. SLATOFF

CORNELL UNIVERSITY

Cornell University Press

ITHACA AND LONDON

International Standard Book Number 0-8014-0580-7
Library of Congress Catalog Card Number 77-123995

Printed in the United States of America
by Vail-Ballou Press, Inc.

*To Joan
and Don*

Preface

MY PURPOSE in the chapters that follow is to point out
some inadequacies of our usual ways of studying and
teaching literature, to insist that books exist primarily to be
read and that they must be read by individual human beings,
and to explore some of the questions which arise when we
do seriously acknowledge that books require readers. I hope
especially to complicate our usual view of involvement,
detachment, and objectivity, and to say something helpful
about the concept of relevance. My intention is to generate
discussion rather than finish it, and what follows must not
be viewed as an effort to cover or even survey systemat-
ically the ground I have ventured onto. I shall be content,
in fact, if I can persuade the reader that there is a ground
to be explored—and perhaps cherished.

I wish to thank my former students James Moody and
Sylvia Lewis for permission to print the final papers they
wrote for my course in Walt Whitman and Emily Dickin-

son; M. H. Abrams, George P. Elliott, and my wife, Jimmy Slatoff, for reading this book in manuscript and making helpful suggestions; and A. R. Ammons for some very important encouragement. I wish to thank also the many friends and colleagues, and above all, my wife, who listened sympathetically as I worried my way through this study.

I am grateful also for the help provided by the Grant-in-Aid Fund of the English Department of Cornell University and by a Humanities Research Grant from the College of Arts and Sciences of Cornell University.

WALTER J. SLATOFF

Ithaca, New York
May 1970

Contents

With Respect
*to Readers*_____
DIMENSIONS OF LITERARY RESPONSE

Chapter 1

In Defense of Readers

ONE FEELS a little foolish having to begin by insisting that works of literature exist, in part, at least, in order to be read, that we do in fact read them, and that it is worth thinking about what happens when we do. Put so blatantly, such statements seem too obvious to be worth making, for after all, no one directly denies that readers and reading do actually exist; even those who have most insisted on the autonomy of literary works and the irrelevance of readers' responses, themselves do read books and respond to them, and many of them make their livings by wrestling with the phenomena which occur as literary works and the minds of students impinge on one another. Equally obvious, perhaps, is the observation that works of literature are important and worthy of study essentially because they can be read and can engender responses in human beings.

Yet certainly if one were to judge from the dominant

modes of literary study and literary theory and from much of the teaching of literature, it would seem as though readers and the act or experience of reading were peripheral if not entirely irrelevant considerations.

I have no desire to denounce the methods and conceptions of the new critics or of modern criticism in general nor to side with those for whom "academic" is a dirty word. Only by viewing literary works as autonomous entities and sets of internal relations can we examine, understand, and enjoy certain of their qualities and obtain certain sorts of clarity and order. And only through the careful and patient study of what may seem minute and trivial matters can we accumulate knowledges we want and need. Moreover, there is no deadline or countdown ahead; we can afford varied approaches and the right of men to explore, however minutely, whatever parts of the landscape they find interesting. Nor is such exploration, as some writers, students, and educational theorists assert, motivated chiefly by insensitivity or pedantry or by the rules that govern academic success and advancement. We have our share of pedants, hacks, and opportunists, and the pressure to publish has provided an alarming quantity of perfunctory, trivial, and unduly specialized work. The chief impetus behind such study, however, is clearly the quest for knowledge. And it is far more often interest and curiosity and enthusiasm than pedantry which lead the individual scholar to dig too long in one spot.

What troubles me and occasions this book is the extent to which certain ways of viewing literature have been accepted as *the* ways to view it, the extent to which the limitations and inadequacies of these ways have been overlooked, and, and, above all, the extent to which certain crucial questions and problems have been ignored or even defined out of existence. It is true that the moment we try to understand literary works in relation to readers we take on troubles which do not arise so long as we look only at the works themselves. For not only is it always more difficult to understand or even talk intelligibly about a process or an interaction than about an object, but a concern with readers seems to lead us into matters of psychology and sociology which we would prefer not to regard as our province. It leads us also, no doubt, into some problems which are essentially insoluble, into waters inherently muddy. Much of the attractiveness of the new criticism and other more or less formalistic approaches is the apparent purity, cleanliness, and scientific precision they seem to allow. If by nothing else, we should be cautioned by literature itself, which surely asserts that science is insufficient, that purity and cleanliness are dangerous and illusory ideals, that to define a problem out of existence will not make it go away, and that human responses always matter.

Most of the limitations and inadequacies of conventional literary study I am going to talk about now are more or less inevitable. I will dwell on them in part because they are often overlooked and in part to point out the need for moving into less hospitable and less familiar realms.

There must always be, I suppose, a distance or discrepancy between actual experience and any effort to think about, talk about, or understand it. If Milton is right, only angels can manage without discursive intellects. And even a Bergson, or Dewey, who would most insist on the dynamic, unitary, inexpressible quality of experience and most emphasize the inadequacies of analysis, must argue his position in the discursive forms whose validity he rejects. But this paradox is particularly acute and troubling in the realm of literary study. For not only is there an enormous gap between the particular kind of experience we undergo when we read and the ways in which we customarily talk about literature, but literature itself, by its very nature, is an assertion of the inadequacy, or at least insufficiency, of analytic ways of talking and knowing. One measure of the peculiar severity of the gap is the extent to which many students resist, first our efforts to make them analyze and organize after they read, and later, in graduate school, our efforts to convert them into scholars. Another measure of it is the frequent distance and even enmity between writers and those who study, teach, or criticize.

Reading even a relatively short and simple poem or story is first of all an action. As one begins to read it, the work is not an object, flat on the table, ready for examination, but rather a territory, sometimes a world, one is about to journey into and explore. As one reads one has the feeling one is moving into and through something and that there is movement within oneself—a succession of varied, complex, and rich mental and emotional states usually involving expectancy, tensions and releases, sensations of anxiety, fear, and discovery, sadness, sudden excitements, spurts of hope, warmth, or affection, feelings of distance and closeness, and a multitude of motor and sensory responses to the movement, rhythm, and imagery of the work as well as a variety of activities and responses—recognition, comparison, classification, judgment, association, reflection—usually spoken of as intellectual. Very few experiences engage one's consciousness in so many ways and give one such a sense that something is going on within oneself. Consider, for example, the immeasurable difference between what goes on in a consciousness while it is fully responding to, say, *King Lear, Moby-Dick,* or *The Wasteland* and the state of that consciousness on most other occasions. If Coleridge is right, the reading of a poem may bring the whole soul into activity.

Even the most immediate, sensitive, perceptive, and rewarding act of reflection after finishing a book inevitably involves some sense of departure from the act of reading, some change in one's relationship with the work. The work may become more meaningful; one may gain new and even more pleasurable or exciting experiences of it and insights into it, but one is no longer engaged in quite the same way. Not only do large portions of the text lose their immediacy and fade, as it were, but one's movement has altered; one is no longer moving through the work in accord with its own moment-to-moment rhythms and contours, but rather in accord with the requirements of whatever lines of inquiry or speculation one is pursuing. This remains true even when reflection makes one more vividly conscious of the work or makes it seem richer and more important than one had realized while reading.

If it were possible for most literary study, criticism, and teaching to consist of the sort of full, immediate, and excited reflection I have just mentioned, reflection still dominated by the recollection and aftereffects of the act of reading, the particular gap I am concerned with would not be much worth worrying about. And certainly some of our study, criticism, and teaching is of this sort. If it were not, far fewer young people would be enticed by our courses and books. Most of it, however, is of a quite different kind. When I say this I am thinking not only of our concern with literary or intellectual history or of the enormous number of studies which focus on a single aspect of some writer or work or which trace a single theme or symbol or idea through a number of authors or works, but of the overwhelming extent to which the literary work is viewed as an object—and to which the purpose of literary study is seen as the fullest description, classification, dissection, and analysis of that object and the investigation of that object's relation to others of its kind. Even those studies which purport to analyze the ways in which a work achieves its effects usually do so in relation to a highly simplified and schematized view of the act of reading. Moreover, their effort is not so much to determine or understand the full effects the work actually does produce as to explain how its organization or patterns can be understood in relation to a few major effects the author or work presumably intends to produce. And even when we seek in our classes to conduct what we sometimes call the "close reading" of a text, we normally view the work as an object to be analyzed rather than as a part of an experience. It is true that we hope such training will lead the student to richer and fuller activity as he reads in the future (and I will comment more fully on this later), but the activity in the classroom is nevertheless closer to what occurs in a scientific laboratory than to the experience of actual reading.[1]

Lengthening the distance between reading and literary study is the fact that reading is a private activity, a relation between the work and a single self. Often it is a very intimate relation, involving the deepest parts of one's being. Yet the study of literature is essentially a public activity; even the smallest and most intimate seminar is a public occasion in which one is talking with relative strangers. We have all smiled or frowned at the naïve young student who complains that analyzing or even talking about a poem "ruins" it, or is like tearing up a flower. The view is naïve and silly insofar as it oversimplifies the nature of both the poem and the act of analysis and values only a personal and usually too narrow experience. But the complaint does point to a real and sometimes objectionable discrepancy between the private and the public activity, and readers who are far from naïve may feel about certain forms of literary study and analysis, or about any analysis of works particularly dear to them, the way one feels about clinical handbooks on sex or marriage or might feel about a detached or public examination of a person one loves. To the extent that the public activity ignores, as it must, some of the deepest and most intimate

[1] For a brilliant and beautiful discussion of the impasses both writers and readers face as the work of art becomes seen and felt as an object and of our deep human needs to find and relate to persons behind and within literary and other objects, see Walter J. Ong, *The Barbarian Within* (New York: Macmillan, 1962), pp. 20–25.

responses, it may be seen not only as incomplete but as irrelevant and even evasive, and like many other public activities, may easily become perfunctory or cynical.

Another general and largely inevitable limitation of literary study is the discrepancy between its usual forms and languages and those of the literary works themselves. Few of us have not at one time or another been dismayed by some particularly vivid example of this discrepancy— a drily statistical account of a rich and flexible literary style, a chatty discussion of an epic or tragedy, a studious and elaborate analysis of a "beat" poem or a pedantic discussion of a poem attacking pedantry, a lengthy and ponderous study of the intellectual or social history presumably implicit in some delicate lyric poem. But these are merely exaggerated instances of a problem inherent in all our work.

One might argue that almost all systems of knowledge are developed and maintained in forms and languages alien to the events and objects they embrace. The knowledge of the mating habits of frogs is one thing and the habits themselves are quite another. The actual decline and fall of the Roman empire and Gibbon's words about it are far from identical. No one expects knowledge of music or painting to be played or painted. With respect to literature, however, the problem is more complex, for literature by its very existence implies the inadequacy or limitations of other forms of verbal discourse. To a large extent we define as literature that writing whose form and language in one way or another transcend the conventional ways of organizing and selecting words, that writing which achieves something more than order and clarity. The writer has chosen something other than the ordinary modes to convey his insights or experience or ideas, and we, by choosing to study literature, assent to the worth and even superiority of his choice. Over and over again we seek to show our students the richness and complexity which the artist has been able to achieve through having made that choice.

Moreover, to the extent that literature relies on metaphor as opposed to inductive and deductive processes, it particularly challenges the kind of logic and clarity and unmysteriousness we usually demand from ourselves and our students and which we normally regard as an indispensable quality of what we call knowledge. As we again try to teach our students, metaphor is irreducible, cannot be translated without loss. One need not go as far as Ransom and others [2] who see an absolute separation or antipathy between scientific and poetic ways of knowing to feel an opposition between the two and to feel uncomfortable about our central reliance as teachers and scholars on other than metaphorical modes of discourse and knowing. Poems themselves, as well as poets, are critical of our work.

The sorts of discrepancies I have just touched upon would be less troubling perhaps if the knowledge we gained through the systematic study of literature were or could be objective, "pure," or independent of such unscientific quantities as readers and acts of reading. There would then be at least a neatness and clarity to the prob-

[2] Simon Lesser, for example, argues that fiction (and I assume he would include poetry) is formed in such a way as to prevent analysis and conceptualization as one reads and that one's performance of these operations would inhibit both response and full understanding (*Fiction and the Unconscious*, [New York: Vintage Books, 1962], p. 154).

lem. But even the most rigid formalist or defender of the autonomy of the literary work, and even the most systematic counter or classifier of images, cannot avoid some contamination, for unless he assumes some kind of reader he has no more reason to study metrical patterns than he has to study the frequency of the letter "p"; no more reason to count and classify images of color than he has to count and classify prepositions or words beginning with the letters "gh." If by nothing else, the would-be literary scientist is contaminated because he himself has probably read the work he is investigating. And even if in some exquisitely misguided pursuit of objectivity he were deliberately to avoid prejudicing himself by reading it, to study works he has not read, his work would still be conditioned by his reading of other works. His very choice to study a literary work rather than a newspaper headline implies a belief in the importance of certain kinds of responses.

The sort of argument I have just been offering may seem unnecessary or even silly, for surely few would defend or pursue such a mechanical ideal of purity. Nevertheless, to the extent that we do reject as irrelevant or even ignore the act of reading we would seem to be pursuing some such ideal. In a sense it is being pursued or at least tacitly accepted by any scholarly or critical study which deliberately ignores the question of how its findings about a work are related to the reader's experience of the work, which fails to consider, for example, whether and how much the archetypes or patterns it has "discovered" communicate.

When confronted directly with the question, very few

scholars or critics would seriously deny that the value of a discovery about a work has some relation to an experiencing of the work. In practice, however, the question is rarely pressed. The usual study is likely to point out how its findings "illuminate" or "explain" the work, but rarely considers how they relate to actual or even hypothetical experiencing of the work. The overall result is that we have an enormous number of pieces of information about literary works with few guides as to their relative importance and no theoretical or practical agreement as to how that importance is to be determined. I am not thinking here of studies which blow up clearly minor aspects of works or "discover" patterns which are the products of mere ingenuity. The problem exists with respect to what we sometimes like to call our body of knowledge. What I am saying is that we have no ways, or at least no agreed-upon ways, of forming our knowledge into a body. We don't know which is heart and which is hands and which is fingernails, and we have so many "seminal" studies that one hesitates to imagine the sort of body they imply.

More worrisome, however, than the incorporeal quality of our knowledge in general, or the limitations of any particular studies, is our persistent unwillingness to face the problem of communication. We are willing neither to adopt a purely formalist position, and thereby to deny the relevance of communication, nor to grapple with the difficulties which arise when we do admit that relevance. Most of the time we proceed as though there were no difficulties.

We rarely concern ourselves, for example, with the

problem of individual differences among readers or even with the question of how much control and guidance of responses is provided by any particular literary work or by literary works in general. On the few occasions we do entertain such questions we speak as though they were settled by reducing response to two categories—appropriate and inappropriate.

We rarely question the value of our pervasive attention to the patterns and unifying aspects of literary works—to recurrences, symmetries, contrasts, correspondences, and tyings together—and do not wonder much about their disorderly, disruptive, and explosive aspects. Little of our work contemplates the extent to which much of our greatest literature involves a disordering as well as an ordering of experience and the extent to which the life and power and even form of a work may come from that disordering or from the very struggle or even failure of the artist to provide order.

We rarely even worry on either a theoretical or practical level about the relationship between the qualities of a work and the perception of those qualities, and for the most part ignore much that philosophers, psychologists, and our own common sense have taught us about the complexities of this relation and the naïveté of ignoring it. Consider, for example, the nature of a fictional character in the work and in the mind. We are fond of insisting on the distinction between real and fictional characters, and of asserting that a fictional character has no existence or verifiable life beyond the information provided by the text. And we smile at the silliness of those who want to argue about how many children Lady Macbeth had or about the sexual problems of Emma Woodhouse. We admit, of course, that some writers are capable of providing a strong illusion of life and we will distinguish between flat and round characters, but we insist that in any responsible discussion a character should be viewed as a verbal construction rather than as a psychological entity or living being. And we are usually terribly impatient with students and critics who insist on confusing the two. There are distinctions to be made, of course, and most students must certainly be taught to pay more attention to the text than they do, but the problem is much trickier than we usually admit.

For one thing, real people are not quite so real and verifiable as we pretend for most practical purposes. Large parts of the lives even of those closest to us—wives, children, friends—are forever blacked out and unverifiable, even unknowable. Parts of our own lives are similarly unverifiable. Nor can we say of ourselves and others where we begin and end, what our limits are. Essentially our sense of a real person, like our sense of a fictional one, is a construction from a relatively limited number of observations of what he says and does. For another thing, we cannot really comprehend a novel or story without giving characters at least some of the attributes of living people, for much of the information we receive about them in the text itself makes it absolutely necessary to imagine that they have ongoing lives even when we aren't watching them. If this were not true they would have to be recreated each time they appeared on the scene. On the most elementary level, we must imagine such a life when we are told something as simple as that Emma Woodhouse "had lived nearly twenty-one years in the world with very little to distress or vex her" or when we are told simply that a character woke up in the morning or went to New York. In a more complex way we are encouraged to imagine a full person when we are told that a character lay awake much of the night, fitfully dreaming, or that Will Ladislaw had a "susceptible temperament—without any neutral region of indifference in his nature, ready to turn everything that befell him into the collisions of a passionate drama." In fact one of the chief efforts of most novelists is to persuade us that their characters are live people. We cannot make any easy division between the work itself and the act of perception or imagination, for the very form and language of the work, so to speak, incorporate or build upon that act.

Or consider the relation between various literary forms and techniques and their actual impact. If one contrasts the techniques by which Joyce's Molly Bloom and Jane Austen's Emma are rendered, or Virginia Woolf's Mrs. Dalloway and Richardson's Pamela, one is struck by the enormous differences, differences so marked and obvious that they hardly seem worth pointing out. One might expect that these differences in technique would lead to immense and profound differences in the reader's sense and conception of the characters, differences as great, say, as between the impacts of a conventional Greek sculpture and one by Lipchitz or Henry Moore. If, however, we examine our responses to these characters, we find that despite important differences, they come to exist for us as much the same sorts of entities; that is, they are similarly immediate, full, and alive. They are very different sorts of people, of course, and we may feel one or another of them to be somewhat more full, round, vivid, complex, or interesting, but the differences in the forms which they take in our consciousness are far less significant than the differences in the forms by which they were presented. This discrepancy is due in part, I think, to our natural tendency to overlook or minimize, while studying them, the common aspects of differing techniques and in part to an inevitable and valid imaginative filling in and fleshing out which we perform as we read. As one reads Molly's interior monologue, which, strictly speaking, is only a transcript of her consciousness, it is impossible not to endow her with other dimensions; indeed her own awareness of her body is such that only a carefully programmed reading machine could fail to feel the presence of that particular dimension of her being. Similarly, as one reads Jane Austen's statements about Emma's behavior and feelings one cannot help but supply an ongoing inner life or stream of consciousness, so to speak. I call this sort of filling in valid and inevitable because if we did not do something of the sort, fictional characters would, in fact, be no more than verbal structures or anatomical and psychological freaks. When an author gives a character a name, he indicates he is creating a person and intends him to be perceived as such; our very use of the word "character" implies that what we experience is a person.

This sort of filling in or rounding out is very different from the loose speculation, daydreaming, or psychologizing about the lives and motives of fictional characters that so irritates anyone who believes that reading must at least be guided and limited by the text. The phenomenon I am talking about is as unavoidable (so long as we read as men and not machines) as our assumption when we hear a voice or see a body that it belongs to a whole person. That this phenomenon does occur, that we must in some respects move beyond the text, of course makes it very difficult to determine just what constitutes a valid reading. Ignoring such responses reduces the difficulty, but also reduces the value and relevance, of our work.

Nor is this kind of inevitable filling in or translation confined to characters. Surely, we do something similar with respect to scenes and atmospheres. If we did not, rooms would often be houseless or lack doors or walls or ceilings; landscapes would often be without skies or horizons. I suspect also that while there would be a considerable difference between a reader's response to the line "the room was deserted" and to the line "the chamber, empty, quiet and forlorn," the difference would not be as dramatic as the apparent differences in the lines themselves. Similarly, we react in curiously flexible ways to temporal descriptions and instructions. A number of skilled readers, for example, are certain that the effect of Faulkner's treatment of the past is to seal it off from the present; other skilled readers are equally certain that what he produces is a sense of the presentness of the past or of the continuity between past and present. All readers, I believe, perform some translation of the past into present when they read a story in the past tense. There is a difference, it is true, between the effect of a work written in the present tense (John walks into the room. He looks steadily at the ground) and the past (John walked into the room. He looked steadily at the ground), but the difference is not really that between present and past, for the events in most works written in the past tense seem to occur just as immediately, are just as much present to us, as the events of those written in the present tense. Indeed they may even seem more immediate since the present tense in fiction may impress us as contrived.

In many other respects also, the relation between technique or form and response is more complex than much of our work assumes. We rarely take into account, for example, that the responses to various qualities of a work may interfere with one another or even cancel one another out. Thus, we will speak as though a work can simultaneously possess a rich and meaningful verbal and thematic texture and a high degree of suspense or hypnotic power without wondering how much the anxious or "hypnotized" reader can attend to nuances or how much a close attention to meanings will inhibit the hypnotic effect. Thus, in our discussions of symbols or imagery we do not often ask how our perception of a particular symbol or image is affected by the intensity of our response to something which precedes or follows it or by the general condition of consciousness generated by one or another of the larger contexts in which it appears. In general, because we speak only of what seem to be properties of the work, we speak as though all effects, regardless of their nature, could be simultaneous.

We usually fail also to consider the changes over time in the effects of particular qualities of a work. Suppose, for example, we are concerned with the significance of the unusual form and structure of a work like *The Sound and the Fury*—the use of an idiot as narrator, the rapid and unsequential temporal shifts, the technique, as Aiken puts it, of "progressive and partial and delayed disclosure." The direct impact of these techniques is undoubtedly greatest upon first reading. If the reader is not simply put off by them, they lead him, I believe, to apprehend the work in a peculiarly disturbed and involved way. A second reading is a quite different experience from the first. There are less mystification, groping, and tension and far more reverberation and illumination as one brings to bear on earlier sections information and awareness gleaned from later ones. And with each successive reading, of course, this process continues until it seems not too much to say that the form and structure have been radically transformed. The very same structures which had served to fragment experience now serve to pull it together.

This is, of course, merely an extreme illustration of something which occurs with the rereading of any work as the effects of sequence and novelty wear off and one gains more and more sense of the work as a spatial entity. Beyond this are the countless subtle alterations of one's experience that occur with each rereading. I am not merely repeating the truism that all experiences are shaped and altered by preceding experiences. Insofar as the literary entity is a structure of relations and emphases and proportions, one must say that the work itself undergoes a transformation as one rereads it. One can, of course, say that the form of the work remains constant and that it is only one's experience of it which changes, and as I have said before we must make such a formulation for certain kinds of clarity, but there is no *human* way of defining that form without assuming some sort of perceiving act.

The sorts of problems I have been raising cannot be re-

limited largely by communal and individual value judgments. We may quarrel over why literature is valuable
and which literature is valuable; we may ignore the question of value in much of our work; but essentially the
entities within our field of professional vision are there because for one or another reason they have been thought
valuable. Moreover, most of us study and teach literature
because we value it and we devote most of our attention to
those writers and works we value most. Even the most
"objective" and impersonal literary history or even an investigation of the most minor influence on the most minor
work of a minor figure is predicated on the notion that
knowledge about literature is valuable because literature is
valuable. That our very "discipline" is rooted in and shaped
by subjective choices inevitably complicates our purposes
and suggests that we can hardly proceed as though we
were scientists exploring natural phenomena.

The objects we study are curious also in that they assume their full or significant form and being only in active
conjunction or interaction with a human mind. To some
extent, of course, this is true of all objects. Whatever one's
theory of perception, one has to agree that some qualities
of any object are dependent on human perception. But
works of literature have scarcely any important qualities
apart from those that take shape in minds.

Most of what I have said so far about the "discipline" of
literary study would hold for the study of any of the arts.
The fields of study are determined by groups of "objects"
—paintings, sculptures, musical scores, and performances—
groups defined largely by value judgments. The objects
themselves (or experiences they occasion) are felt to be

valuable for their own sakes and they take their significant shape only in human minds. (The oversimplification of this description and the important differences between the arts do not, I think, affect my point here.) And of course, students of the fine arts and music have wrestled with many of the same sorts of problems that we have in defining their purposes and directions. But again there are important differences. Even if some would quarrel with my conviction that language is inherently a more complex medium than paints or musical sounds, there can be no doubt that works of literature confront us far more acutely than do paintings or musical compositions with questions having to do with ideas, beliefs, attitudes, and meaning, questions which cannot be managed by formal analysis or aesthetic theory and which force us inevitably into realms beyond the grasp of our own or any other specialty.

In short, so long as we allow literature itself to shape our activities, and are unwilling to betray its curiously complex nature, which is chiefly why we value it so highly, our pursuit cannot become a discipline in the usual sense of the term; we cannot organize our activities under a single or entirely coherent rubric. If in the interest of order we define our field as communications we convert magnificent individual objects into samples and by-products. To limit our concern to literary history or formal analysis on the other hand, to ignore problems of value and human response, is to ignore the very qualities of literature which have led us to be concerned with it in the first place.

So long as we are unwilling to oversimplify and distort the nature of literature we shall have to live as individuals and function as departments of literature with the strains of trying to adjust knowledge and appreciation, of trying to be good scholars and good readers. These strains are greater than we normally admit in catalogues, to students, or at faculty meetings. We are fond of pointing out the many ways in which knowledge and scholarship illuminate literature and can enrich the reader's experience; we are less fond of keeping in view the conflicts—the sorts of discrepancies between study and reading discussed earlier in this chapter, the differences between the kinds of detachment, objectivity, narrowing of interest and focus required in scholarship and the kinds of sympathy, engagement, general responsiveness and openness, and emotional susceptibility involved in good reading. Scholarship must always require some degree of specialization of both knowledge and interest, a requirement which in our time, as we all know, daily becomes more and more extreme. Fully responsive reading requires breadth of knowledge and interest. As individuals and members of departments we face the difficult task of pursuing specialities without becoming specialists. If we become mere specialists, if we behave as though the reading and study of literature were the province of specialists, we pervert the very nature, substance, and value of the thing we study and cut off all routes back to its center.

The position I am urging is by no means a comfortable or entirely attractive one. It calls not for an easy eclecticism but for a recognition of strains and conflicts inherent in both the theory and practice of our work; it asks that we stop trying to define away mysteries and problems and grapple with them instead; it chooses confusion over the order of oversimplification. And it confronts us with questions which we scarcely know how to talk about. My purpose in the pages which follow is simply to ask some of these questions and to begin talking about them.[3]

[3] The reader will find that I have very little to say about one crucial aspect of the reader's experience—his unconscious responses. Unquestionably such responses are important and need study. I say little about them here in part because I do not understand much about them, in part because I wanted to limit myself to matters which could be examined without specialized knowledges and terminologies, and in part because two excellent books have already been written on the subject: Simon Lesser's *Fiction and the Unconscious* and, more recently, Norman Holland's *The Dynamics of Literary Response* (New York: Oxford University Press, 1968).

Chapter 2

Varieties of
Involvement

I WANT to worry first about some dimensions of the literary experience that have received so little investigation that I scarcely know how to begin. The area is suggested but not defined by the questions: In what sense is reading a personal activity? What kinds of involvement does reading entail? Where can we move or stand between or beyond the equally unsatisfactory positions of the aesthetic theorists who insist that one's relation to a work of art both can and should be impersonal and detached and who argue that personal responses are irrelevant and even contaminating, and those who argue that the only valid and important responses are what they call personal ones?

It would be naïve to expect that we will ever achieve very satisfactory understanding of a matter which draws in the concepts of objectivity and subjectivity and lies finally in the mystery of man's perception and comprehension of any external object or event. But we can do better than we have. If nothing else, we might throw out the arbitrary maps and recognize the complexity of the terrain.

In two very obvious senses actual reading is always a personal activity. It is an act performed by an individual person and the experience occurs within the mind and sensibilities of an individual person. Not only is the act personal, but one has the sense that it is, and draws satisfaction in part because, unlike most of our activities, it is personal, a kind of being with oneself, albeit in a peculiarly rich and exciting way. One is alone, yet in intimate relationship with something else. It combines some of the pleasures of solitary drinking, friendship, introspection, keyhole peeping, drug taking, walking, and puzzle doing. Moreover, the experience is not only personal but private in that it is essentially invisible to others and cannot be fully communicated.

One can explore works in seminars and discussion groups, one can attend to and make use of the experiences and observations of others, and gain new insights and ways of responding, but a reading, and the insights and responses, for that matter, can occur only in an individual consciousness. There is nowhere else for them to occur. This is true not only of the moment-to-moment sequential movement through the work that we usually call reading, but of the fuller experience of it that comes from repeated readings or patient exploration.

These statements seem innocuous enough until we recall that they throw the problem of defining full or proper response or full understanding back within the limits of individual consciousness. There, if one is not merely to be a storehouse, all the relevant responses and awarenesses that groups and critics need only accumulate and point to must come into relation and interact with one another. There, if it is to occur at all, must take place that mysterious fusion of knowledge, judgment, sensory comprehension, and emotional response toward which we hope our teaching and scholarship labor. But there, even apart from individual differences, the experience will always involve a selectivity, an incredibly complex distribution between the centers of attention and emotion and the peripheries. There certain responses will by their intensity inevitably diminish, blur, or entirely inhibit others. There, on the other hand, an effort to respond to or be aware of too many aspects of a work may prevent intensities of focus and concentration which are also required by the work. There, responses are not merely appropriate or proper or valid or informed or educated, but possess textures, colors, and relative degrees of intensity and depth and significance that we can scarcely begin to describe, much less prescribe, in proper proportion. Consider, for example, the difficulty in defining what might be called a "sufficient" or "full" response to any particular work. I am not yet talking about individual differences, but merely the complexity and mystery of any good reader's experience per se, the sense in which reading is personal because it is done by the single consciousness of a person rather than by a group or a machine or a library, or by the ideal reader sometimes invoked as a critical aid.

When we begin to contemplate the extent to which individual differences shape literary experiences it becomes understandable why we have clutched so desperately at theories and ways of talking which permit us to ignore those differences and have tried to relegate them to provinces labeled "psychology" or "taste." On the sensory level alone, our experiences differ more from one another than it is comfortable to reckon with. We differ not only in the thresholds of response of our various senses (in what might be called "innate sensitivity"), but in the prominence of our senses in relation to one another. Some readers are moles; others are transparent eyeballs. Some readers have a virtual painting in their heads as they read the words "a pair of ragged claws / Scuttling across the floors of silent seas." Others are most acutely aware of the sounds. Still others experience chiefly a kinesthetic scuttling. Probably no two readers experience the rhythms, sounds, and images of a poem in precisely the same proportions. And as I. A. Richards and others have pointed out, we vary remarkably in the extent to which we feel and think in images of any sort. Some readers can scarcely apprehend anything without forming quite specific images of some variety. Others apparently can have rich and detailed experience employing only the sketchiest images, if any at all.[1] This does not imply that we cannot educate our senses to greater awareness or ought not to try to attune them as much as possible to the intent of the particular work. It does mean, however, that the apprehension of a work is to an important extent personal and that

[1] For more detailed discussion of these and other sensory matters, see I. A. Richards, *Principles of Literary Criticism* (London: Routledge & Kegan Paul Ltd., 1926), pp. 92–133, and his *Practical Criticism* (London: Routledge & Kegan Paul Ltd., 1929), pp. 235–236, 362–364.

while we might talk sensibly of a normal range and proportion of sensory responses to any work and class some responses as inappropriate, we cannot talk meaningfully about an ideal or correct sensory response. Nor can we suppose that when any two readers have learned to give the same nomenclature, say, to Hopkins' rhythms and sounds, they are having the same experience of them. It suggests, too, that some of our tastes, preferences, and even evaluations may well be grounded in these personal sensory differences and that it might be worth trying to find out something about how large a part they play in such choices.[2] Something of their role and their variation is suggested by the extent to which we find such variations among writers themselves.

If one is to experience the rhythms, sounds, and images of a work, and not merely to identify them in accordance with a crude and only moderately expedient nomenclature, one simply cannot leave one's particular sensory organization behind. No matter how much one respects the liter-

---

[2] Such an inquiry, of course, faces obvious difficulties and can lead to such atrocities as hooking up subjects to elaborate electrical apparatus. But, as with most questions, if we attend to the matter, we can get somewhere through careful self-examination and careful questioning of others. It would not be too difficult, for example, to discover something interesting about one's own or another's intensities and proportions of visual, aural, and kinesthetic response to such lines as "The plowman homeward plods his weary way," "The woods are lovely, dark, and deep," or "Over the bent world broods with warm breast and with ah! bright wings." And one might, by examining responses to a few more carefully chosen lines, discover degrees of sensitivity to (and delight in) particular varieties of alliteration and assonance or to marked or sudden caesurae.

ary work itself, and how diligently one seeks to experience *its* shape and emphases, no matter how well one learns to control one's aberrant or idiosyncratic sensory responses, the reading must be an engagement between the work and a particular organism.

When we go beyond the sensory level and consider our variations in sex, age, experience, values, attitudes, temperaments, and habits of mind, conscious and unconscious, to say nothing of the variations in both the conscious and unconscious purposes for which we read—all of which go into shaping and proportioning our experience of a work—it seems wonderful that we can achieve as much communication and agreement as we do about the meaning and worth of any particular work. One might consider, as a single example, the inevitable differences in the response to King Lear's predicament of a confident eighteen-year-old and a weary old man, of a bachelor and a married man, of a daughter who feels close to her father and one who doesn't, of a man who has experienced and recognized a serious betrayal and one who hasn't, of an equable man and a hot-tempered one, to say nothing of the minor differences which might occur between any two people in any one of those categories. Or if one begins to think about the limits of a "proper" or even "adequate" response or experience, one might wonder whether such an experience would be possible for either an unshaken eighteen-year-old or an old man who had just been disowned by his children, a man who is in Lear's shoes, so to speak. Such a man might well feel unbearably involved in and moved by the play; but would he be responding to *Lear's* predicament? I hope to show later that the answer to this question is less obvious than it has usually seemed. My intent here is simply to emphasize the importance of individual differences.

Despite this bewildering variety of individual response we do, of course, manage a considerable degree of communication. We achieve this, in part, by learning to submit ourselves as much as possible to the work itself, by letting our responses be directed and limited as much as possible by it, and, in part, by restricting our discussion largely to those matters about which we can communicate easily or what we sometimes call objectively. This is fine and we must never stop trying to do it. Otherwise we invite and celebrate chaos. At the same time, however, we must recognize how much we oversimplify and disregard by this procedure and try to find ways of moving intelligibly into the disregarded territories. Most important, we need to stop pretending that the sort of discussion we do have at all covers the total ground of our experience of a book.

One measure of how far we have to go is the fact that virtually no critic even admits—in print, at any rate—that his reading of a work may in any way be affected by his own nature, experience, training, temperament, values, biases, or motive for reading. Another measure is the incredible crudity of our language when we do venture to talk about readers' responses. Scholars and critics who would distinguish carefully between various sorts of Neo-Platonism, or examine in minute detail the structure of a chapter or the transmutations of a prevailing metaphor, or trace the full nuances of a topical allusion, will settle happily for mere labels like distance, involvement, identification, detachment, emotional impact, intensity, powerful effect, sympathetic, unsympathetic, deeply felt—labels just about as precise as the term "romantic." Apart from brief general discussions of "Objective and Subjective" and "Connotation and Denotation" and a very brief comment on "Empathy and Sympathy," M. H. Abrams' excellent *A Glossary of Literary Terms* has almost no entries which refer directly to matters of readers' responses. An even more recent glossary contains not a single such entry.

I have no new terminology or full-blown theory to propose. But I would like to begin to look more closely at some of these loosely labeled areas of response. Before we can even begin to look, however, we must try to escape from a set of related polarities and dichotomies which have seriously limited our thinking and observation: objective-subjective, clear thinking-emotional involvement, judgment-sympathy, impersonal-personal, accurate-impressionistic, knowledge-appreciation. In each of these polarities and others like them an activity associated with emotion, feeling, or involvement is seen as some kind of distortion or enemy of proper understanding. Very often the "subjective" pole is equated with irresponsibility and self-indulgence. Now, we need not settle the ultimate questions about the nature of reality and man's perception of it to recognize that such dichotomies and value judgments are particularly inadequate and inappropriate for understanding responses to literature. For one thing, literary works, unlike natural objects, are designed to affect the emotions and to compel various sorts of involvement. Conrad, for example, views the artist as one who "speaks to our capacity for delight and wonder, to the sense of mystery surrounding our lives; to our sense of pity, and beauty, and pain; to the latent feeling of fellowship with all creation—and to the subtle but invincible conviction of solidarity that knits together the loneliness of innumerable hearts, to the solidarity in dreams, in joy, in sorrow, in aspirations, in illusions, in hope, in fear, which binds men to each other." He goes on to say that the "task which I am trying to achieve is, by the power of the written word to make you hear, to make you feel—it is above all, to make you *see*." [3] Coleridge wished poetry to bring the whole soul of man into activity. Scarcely a writer or critic has doubted—in words at any rate—that literature aims to involve something approaching man's whole being.

Moreover, the very meaning of a literary work depends on emotional responses. Most works could scarcely be comprehended at all by a reader who lacked all human emotions. Nor are emotional responses inherently less responsible than intellectual ones. One can read as irresponsibly intellectually as one can emotionally, exploit a text to satisfy intellectual needs as easily as to satisfy emotional ones. To respect a text doesn't mean to read impersonally or unemotionally any more than to respect another person means holding him at arm's length. Respect demands a giving of self and bringing of self to bear.

All this seems to obvious to be worth saying until one recalls the incredible extent to which those who care about art have overreacted in act and theory to the general public's tendency to celebrate and trust only emotional response and recalls the strength of the view that finds it a worthy activity to dwell on intellectual responses to a

[3] "Preface," *The Nigger of the Narcissus, Conrad's Prefaces* (London: J. M. Dent & Sons, 1937), pp. 50, 52.

work and a self-indulgence to savor emotional ones. Again and again we are told to think and worry about the prevalence and dangers of inappropriate responses—about the naïve playgoer who rushes onstage to strangle Iago, about the reader who likes or dislikes a character or portrait because the character reminds him of his Aunt Sally, about the unworthiness of books which leave one feeling one ought to join an organization or write a check. From my colleagues I have heard ten thousand stories of their students' foolish and inappropriate responses and I have told many such stories of my own. Rarely does one hear a word about the danger of insufficient responses—about the playgoer who never even feels like rushing onstage, about the reader who never lets a character or work connect in any way with his personal experience, about the reader who never feels guilty or never re-examines himself or his responsibilities after finishing a book, about those for whom literary works have become little more than puzzles, games, historical items, or storehouses of images, symbols, myths, or archetypes. Scarcely a word has been addressed to the problem of what in general or specific instances constitutes a full or adequate as opposed to merely appropriate response. Until the subjective, personal, and emotional are seen as inevitable and essential parts of reading and not as intrusions and fallacies, the problem cannot even be recognized. Nor can we begin to talk meaningfully about what does go on or should go on in the actual encounter between a man and a book.

The single most important thing to observe about our emotional transactions with a literary work is that they do not occur along single continuums nor are they in accord with the dimensions of any one metaphor. Even the most limited reader is capable of maintaining several simultaneous states of relation and feeling toward a work, and most readers could say with André Gide that they "have the gift of combining at the same moment two states of mind as different, as contradictory, as passion and lucidity, or as the fever, the delirium, the inward tremor or lyricism, and the chill of reason." [4] Most of us can simultaneously react, identify, and empathize and watch and even feel ourselves doing so. At one and the same moment we can be moved enough to weep and remain cool enough to fight the tears or to be ashamed of them. We can share the experience of a Gulliver, say, feel that experience, and at the same time view him with detachment and view with detachment the part of ourselves that is identifying. We can sympathize with a character despite an author's clear indications that we are not to do so, recognize this, and go on sympathizing. We are just as capable of juxtaposing and keeping in suspension feelings as we are ideas.

It has been recognized, of course, though by no means widely enough, that much reading does put the reader in a generally dual condition of being at once a participant in the action and a detached spectator of it. [5] And there has been quite extensive and thoughtful discussion of the

[4] Roger Martin du Gard, *Recollections of André Gide* (New York: The Viking Press, 1953), p. 96; quoted in Bacon and Breen, *Literature as Experience* (New York: McGraw-Hill, 1959), p. 48.

[5] See, for example, Simon Lesser, *Fiction and the Unconscious* (New York: Vintage Books, 1962), pp. 142–143; Bacon and Breen, pp. 48–49.

complexities of the unconscious and "primitive" aspects of our participation in literary works. But there has been little recognition, even on the part of these psychologically oriented critics, of the multiplicities and complexities of our involvement in a work or of the inadequacies of our usual concept of a detachment-involvement continuum or of a distance continuum.[6] Most people and most critics, when they touch upon the matter at all, speak as though detachment and involvement were simple opposites and as though readers were simply more or less involved or detached or more or less distant. Apart from its failure to recognize the reader's ability to experience multiple or opposing responses in this respect, such a view lumps together under the label "involvement" a variety of qualitatively different literary experiences. It fails, if nothing else, to distinguish between an experience which simply arouses one's emotions, that is, in which one responds emotionally, and an experience entailing some kind of personal participation in the story or characters. Obviously these experiences are not always easy to separate, but surely we are sometimes moved deeply by characters and events we are

[6] I am grateful to Douglas Park, a graduate student of mine, for calling my attention to one article which does indeed recognize some of these multiplicities and complexities: D. W. Harding's "Psychological Processes in the Reading of Fiction," *British Journal of Aesthetics*, II (1962), 133–147. Harding relates the role and responses of readers to those of listeners to gossip and those of onlookers at actual events. He concludes that the terms "identification" and "vicarious experience" designate too great a variety of responses to be very useful and points out some of the ways in which readers both imaginatively share the experience of characters and at the same time, or immediately afterward, contemplate them as fellow beings.

essentially observing from the outside and surely this kind of experience can be quite different from the involvement that comes through empathy and identification. In the first instance, one may say that one feels an emotion, say pity, and thereby becomes involved. In the second, one becomes involved and thereby experiences the emotion. But even this division is grossly inadequate, as I shall try to show in a few moments.

The single continuum fails also to make an important distinction between a high degree of something we might call attention or fascination (a condition in which we might describe ourselves as engrossed, carried away, absorbed, gripped, etc.) and a condition of real caring or real concern. These may sometimes go hand in hand, but not necessarily. A high degree of suspense, for example, or of primitive identification, may cause one to read with intense anxiety and concentration, may blot out all one's sense of anything but the world of the book (as in a good detective thriller), and in that sense "involve" one; but one may still in important ways feel utterly unconnected with the characters and events; one cares desperately, but not deeply. On the other hand, one may read a novel like *Middlemarch* or *The Ambassadors* with far greater sense of distance, and yet feel deeply and inextricably involved in the events and characters, be far less gripped or carried away than by the thriller, but far more deeply moved. One might try to explain this sort of difference by saying that the thriller provides more primitive, childlike, unconscious, and therefore superficially more powerful sorts of participation or empathy or identification while the more sophisticated works lead to more mature and conscious and therefore more controlled and restrained connections, but I suspect this is at best a small part of the explanation.

The single dimension of involvement or distance fails also to allow for distinctions between sympathy and empathy or implies that empathy is the more "involved" state of the two, an implication by no means necessarily true. In one case my viscera and muscles are involved; in the other my mind and heart. In Faulkner's *Absalom, Absalom!*, for example, I am intensely involved in an empathetic way as Quentin and Shreve themselves empathize with the galloping Charles Bon and Henry Sutpen to the point where no longer four but two are galloping alone; but I am much more fully and deeply shaken and involved at the end when poor Quentin cries out his ambivalence toward the South. At this point I experience some empathy from Faulkner's emphasis on Quentin's panting but surely the chief and most powerful feeling is one of sympathy toward a bewildered and suffering creature who is very clearly not myself.

Nor does the simple continuum help us to distinguish between empathy, which is essentially a lending of oneself to the character, and projection, which is a substitution of the self or part of the self for the character. These responses might seem alike insofar as both can be called forms of identification and both involve a loss of distance and detachment; yet, as I hope will be entirely clear later, they represent very different kinds of experience and relation to the work.

We might distinguish also between what could be labeled "voyeuristic" and "anodynic" involvements, between feeling a delicious personal excitement as a tormented character like Eugene Gant bloodies his fists against the wall of his bedroom and feeling how wonderful it is to be such a suffering hero. The voyeur does not so much share the character's experience as watch it, feed upon it, and use it to activate passions and sensations of his own. Despite the intensity of his response and its intimate connection with what he is observing (which leads one to use the term "involvement"), he is in some respects quite cold and detached. "Anodynic" involvement is closer to the activity of imagining oneself dead in order to enjoy the pain of the bereaved and forgetting that death would preclude such enjoyment. In such involvement one forgets that it hurts to suffer and that one will not be contemplating one's own suffering but experiencing it. In neither of these sorts of "involvement" is there much sympathy or recognition of the "otherness" of the characters being observed. Like projection, and unlike empathy and sympathy, these two forms of "involvement" would seem to be exploitations of works rather than experiences of them, since the reader's attention is on himself rather than on the work. And such responses would seem to be inappropriate since few writers or works—few good ones at any rate—presumably intend such effects. Yet one need not go all the way to De Sade to find moments of content and tone which announce the author's own voyeuristic involvement and compel one's own. One can find such moments, surely, in Flaubert, Dostoevsky, Dickens, Conrad, Kafka, Faulkner, Greene, and Nabokov, to name only a few. Nor is it merely the reader's own romanticism that leads him to stand too comfortably in the shoes of such characters as Eugene Gant, Paul Morel, Stephen Dedalus, and Jake

Barnes, for in each case the author is proud of the fact that his semi-autobiographic hero has suffered so much and invests the suffering with a kind of glamor that encourages the reader to overlook the painfulness of the pain.

We might distinguish also between involvements in which the reader experiences a sense of support or nourishment and those in which he or his faiths or values are threatened. Most works, no doubt, instill some degree of anxiety, conscious or unconscious, but surely there is an enormous difference between that warm rush of assent we are likely to feel in the symphony chapter of *Moby-Dick* as Ahab for a moment yearns for human connection and the quality of our assent as he casts his final spear, or between our experience as Macomber finally stands up to the lion and our experience as Ole Anderson turns his face to the wall. And there is an enormous difference in the way it feels vicariously to inhabit the worlds, say, of *Middlemarch* and *Vanity Fair* or even *Jude the Obscure* or *Ulysses*, in which we at least know where we are, and the mystifying worlds of *The Castle*, *The Waves*, or *Catch-22*, to say nothing of those produced by Beckett, Burroughs, or Barthelme. Another distinction of special contemporary relevance would be one between the more usual sorts of identification, concern, sympathy, and empathy and a condition in which one feels not merely involved but implicated or accused, as one does in Brecht's *Threepenny Opera* or Genet's *The Blacks*. In these last cases, we should note, we are involved not at all through a loss of self or distance but as ourselves and as spectators.

The foregoing are but a few of the cruder distinctions

which might be made and explored,[7] and they, themselves, are unsatisfactory insofar as they are dichotomous and classificatory rather than descriptive. The important thing is not to name them but to stop using a simple scale so that the actual experiences, whatever they are, can be talked about in whatever terms prove most appropriate or illuminating.

As may already have become apparent, perhaps the most serious difficulty with the notion of a continuum from detachment to involvement, as well as with the whole concept of aesthetic distance, is that it obscures the fascinating question of the place of self and self-awareness with respect to involvement and detachment.

Traditional aesthetic theory makes a division between a normal workaday state of mind in which we presumably look at things solely in terms of their relationship to ourselves and our needs and an aesthetic state of mind or attitude in which we contemplate objects for what they are in themselves, in which we are presumably detached, objective, impersonal, uninvolved. One can see the logic in such a division, and yet in some respects the dichotomy seems not only an oversimplification but almost the reverse of the actual case. It seems to me that our normal condition is one in which we use objects and people but are not really involved with them or in relation to them, for we are not in possession of ourselves. We and they are parts

[7] How numerous both the varieties and degrees of involvement can be even for a single work will be apparent to anyone who reflects on his experience, say, of Faulkner's *As I Lay Dying* or Ford's *The Good Soldier*.

of a machine or an activity. If I am busy I may be unconscious of my companion's grimace of pain, but I will probably also be unaware of my own headache. If I happen to look out of the window and notice a tree, I see that tree as an object utterly separate from me, objectively, with detachment. It is irrelevant to my activity and to me. Or if I see it and think I could sell it for lumber, I am seeing it in relation to my needs but not in relation to myself. It is when I am contemplating it, just looking at it, really *seeing* it, its shape, color, texture, etc., that I am most aware of my own relation to it. I am not merely looking at it, but am feeling the act of observing it, am acutely aware of where I am in relation to it both physically and psychically. Similarly, if I adopt what is called the aesthetic attitude toward, let us say, a student sitting in my office taking an exam, I am more aware not only of his shape and movements, but of my own presence, location, state of being, and relation to him. Part of the awareness in both cases, it is true, is a sense of distance or separation from the object contemplated, but it is the distance or separation between *us*. I am very much there, very much involved, more involved in a sense than when I am busy giving him directions.

Moreover, I suspect that the fullest and deepest experiences of literary involvement may bring about a heightened sense of self. While reading *Parktilden Village* by George P. Elliott, a novel which particularly compelled my deepest attention, identification, empathy, and emotional and intellectual involvement, I was acutely conscious that I was lying on the floor in my own living room, that I was brimming with anxiety and emotion, and that I was deeply and frighteningly implicated—all this at the same time that I was attending with special care to the characters and events in the book. Unquestionably, much of the power of the experience resided in some terrible tension between my involvement and self-awareness. Perhaps part of the explanation for this sort of phenomenon is that when one is powerfully moved, one's attention is drawn to oneself by the very sensation of being moved, the tightening of the heart or the gathering of tears, which is happening in the self rather than in the book. I suspect something similar occurs even in the most physical or physiological sorts of empathy, that as one vaults with the pole vaulter or gathers one's forces with the discus thrower, one is more conscious of the state of one's own body than when one watches with what is normally thought of as detachment.

A fuller explanation, however, of these complex combinations of involvement and self-consciousness surely has to do with fundamental relations between separation and connection that single-continuum notions of distance and involvement fail to take into account. On the very simplest level, one might say that one can't connect with something one isn't separate from. The very notion of connection or involvement implies some separation, some distance to be crossed. In fact, in many instances when there is connection, the sense of its poignance or importance increases as the distance increases. Thus absence makes the heart grow fonder; thus a handclasp or embrace over barbed wire or at the moment of death is peculiarly powerful. Thus when a writer wishes to establish an especially strong sense

47

of connection he may magnify or stress the distance which has been crossed. Faulkner does this with particular frequency and effect.

You know again now that there is no time: no space: no distance: . . . there is the clear undistanced voice as though out of the delicate antenna-skeins of radio, further than empress's throne, than splendid insatiation, even than matriarch's peaceful rocking chair, across the vast instantaneous intervention, from the long long time ago: *"Listen, stranger, this was myself: this was I."* [8]

Thus lonely romantics like Thomas Wolfe's Eugene Gant or George Webber are likely to feel they are most poignantly involved with mankind when they are looking at it from behind the separation of a train window, and a character like Stephen Dedalus is most likely to experience epiphanies when he is feeling most lonely and isolated. On the most purely physical level, one cannot even see an object or being one has no distance from. If one has taken the place of the object (fully identified with it) or is even shoved right up against it, it ceases to be visible. A somewhat similar inability to see can occur when distance has been sharply reduced by familiarity or even love, as happens sometimes between husband and wife and as is recognized only when some form of separation has brought them into focus for each other, as separate and distinct beings. Other sorts of closeness to an object can reduce as well as heighten one's sense of relation with it. Witness the effect of some Degas paintings or movie close-ups of

[8] *Requiem for a Nun* (New York: Random House, 1950), pp. 261–262.

a kiss or sexual act, or the effect of the undistanced descriptions of a writer like Zola. Or consider Gulliver's feelings as he gazes into the cavernous pores of the Brobdingnagian maiden's breast. The microscope, so to speak, can increase psychic distance at the same time that it, in effect, reduces physical distance. It may be that the revulsion we feel at some of these sorts of close-ups is more akin to empathy than detachment, but in other respects the experience hardly seems one of connection and closeness. It may well be that we are most likely to feel closest to objects and people in some sort of middle distance.

On a somewhat different plane, what I am saying is that many important kinds of involvement require, and even derive from, a sense of self and a recognition that the other is not-me. (One could, I suppose, call this recognition a form of detachment, but only if we come to understand that detachment is not an opposite of involvement and remove from the word its connotations of disinterest, coldness, and impersonality.) Paradoxically, such a recognition can allow one more fully to understand and even share another's plight and point of view, as it exists for him, than the unself-conscious participation or projection that often passes for involvement.

It can even be argued, and has been so argued by John Bayley [9] and others, that true connection, or love, can only occur when the otherness and separateness of the object is fully recognized, and that writers like Chaucer, Shakespeare, and Dickens, who are in one sense detached from and separate from their characters, love them, while writers

[9] *The Characters of Love: A Study in the Literature of Personality* (New York: Basic Books, 1961).

49

like Lawrence and Thomas Wolfe, who seem to be more deeply involved in their characters, exhibit only self-love since their characters are mainly projections of themselves. The same might be said for readers.

If what I am saying is true, if the fullest being-within, for author and reader alike, requires a simultaneous being-without, the distinctions between involvement and detachment, between empathy and sympathy, and even between sympathy and judgment become less pronounced. Not only can they occur simultaneously but harmoniously as well. Shakespeare can be Lear and at the same time pity and judge him, and so can the reader. Merely to be Lear would be neither to see him or know him nor even to be involved with him.

Anyone with children who doubts our capacity for these intense double relations might consider what happens when one sees one's own child being hurt. One feels the pain as though it were one's own and is, I suppose, as fully involved emotionally as it is possible to be. Yet one immediately uses one's separateness and adult self to offer help and one is acutely conscious of the separate selves and of the connection between them.

In general, I think, psychologists, aestheticians, and critics alike have assumed too easily that intense caring or emotional concern comes only from some form of identification or projection, some form of participation, as it were, and have underestimated our capacity to be deeply concerned about, anxious about, and moved by the predicaments of others without performing any act of identification. It may be that the little child initially learns to feel sympathy for another hurt creature by imagining himself in the same condition, and it may be that the only way one can teach people to be more sympathetic is to help them to imagine themselves in other's shoes, but I think that many of us become capable of responding sympathetically without performing that intermediate act (or if we do perform it, we do it so automatically and unconsciously as to make it unrecognizable). Just as few of us would remain unmoved if we were merely to hear the sound of groaning or weeping or of joyous laughter coming from an unknown creature in an adjacent room, a creature whom we have no means of identifying or identifying with, so most of us can be moved by and concerned about the evidences of the emotional states of fictional characters without in any way sharing or experiencing these conditions. And I think most of us become capable of moving directly from an intellectual comprehension of a character's predicament to an actual feeling of sympathy for him. As we come to understand, for example, the full dimensions of Casaubon's plight in *Middlemarch*, we learn, as Dorothea does, to feel for him as we might toward some pathetic "lamed creature," and we are terribly glad that she has not, so to speak, struck him, but rather taken his hand. Few of us, however, in any way, could be said to identify with Casaubon. I am not even sure that the deeper sympathy we feel in that scene for Dorothea depends on anything which we could properly call identification.

Perhaps much of the confusion and oversimplification in this area have come about because no distinction is ever made between identifying with a character and seeing or feeling something from his point of view. Few would deny that we can understand the point of view of another without identifying with him, but there seems to have been no recognition that we are also capable of feeling from another's point of view without in any real sense becoming that character. This may seem to be a quibble in that one might define identification as including any act of perception from another's point of view or might say that identification merely means the seeing and feeling of another's point of view. But I think not only that the distinction is valid psychologically—that it directs attention to two quite distinct sorts of experience (I identify with Marlow; I feel for and with Lord Jim)—but that it also has profound implications of several sorts. If the only way we can deeply comprehend or feel the experience of another is through identification, our range of response is limited by our ability to empathize; if we can feel for and with merely by understanding another's predicament and point of view we can probably have a wider range of experience. A limitation of many readers is that they can only sympathize when they do identify and covet only vicarious experience. If one can feel for another without having to put *oneself* in his shoes or without doing unto him as one would wish done unto oneself, one can perhaps know better what it is like for *him* to be in his shoes and what *he* would like done unto *himself*. This notion is similar, of course, to Bayley's insistence that true connection or love can only occur when the otherness and separateness of the object are fully recognized and accepted.

Another source of difficulty in discussing these matters is the sharp dichotomy which is often made between intellectual and emotional involvement and the implication that involvement is essentially an emotional matter. We can sometimes think without feeling and feel without thinking and the two do frequently get in each other's way; but more often our experiences are deeply interwoven mixtures of the two. At the very least we know that we often think something because we feel something and feel something because we think something, and we are about as hard put to know which came first as we are with the chicken and the egg. We know also that we can care deeply, even violently, about ideas, and I think few would disagree with John Dewey's assertion that "different ideas have their different 'feels,' their immediate qualitative aspects, just as much as anything else. One who is thinking his way through a complicated problem finds direction on his way by means of this property of ideas." Moreover, most good literature is designed to engage, and does engage, both mind and emotion and does engender responses in which thought and feeling are particularly inseparable. I cannot say in *Middlemarch*, for example, and would not wish to, to what extent I care deeply about Dorothea because of my interest in the ethical and moral questions with which she and the novel are concerned and to what extent I care deeply about those questions because of my interest in Dorothea. As nearly as I can tell, the two are inextricably mingled and my very attempt to distinguish between them sounds silly.

A more helpful distinction, if we had some way of making it, might be one which got at the extent to which a response or experience—whether intellectual or emotional —was a full and significant interaction with the work; which got at how much of the reader's being was involved and how significantly, at the extent to which the reader would properly be described as having had an experience as opposed to a mere passing encounter or exercise. And neither a rush of tears nor a rush of thought nor a solemnly pontificated "How true!" or "How tragic!" in itself proves that more than an encounter has taken place. To attempt to define in a general way what might be called full and significant interaction is probably futile and pointless, but we can say that it is something more than either a carefully controlled intellectual response or an emotional orgy, and that, if it is to be achieved, literary works must be viewed as something more than mental and emotional gymnasiums.

One further source of difficulty has been the tendency of most aestheticians and critics to speak as though there were only two sorts of readers: the absolutely particular, individual human being with all his prejudices, idiosyncrasies, personal history, knowledge, needs, and anxieties, who experiences the work of art in solely "personal" terms, and the ideal or universal reader whose response is impersonal and aesthetic. Most actual readers, except for the most naïve, I think, transform themselves as they read into beings somewhere between these extremes. They learn, that is, to set aside many of the particular conditions, concerns, and idiosyncrasies which help to define them in everyday affairs, but they still retain the intellectual and emotional experience and structures, and the temperaments and values, of particular individuals and respond largely in accord with that make-up. When I read, for example, the self that responds is not quite Walter J. Slatoff, Professor of English, third-generation mostly assimilated Jew, aged 48, married, father of Joan and Donald, aged 18 and 16, soldier in World War II, etc., etc. And that self which reads does not say I sympathize with Jake Barnes because I know what war is like but resent Hemingway's treatment of Cohn because I, too, am Jewish and in other ways resemble Cohn more than I do Jake. But at the same time, that reading self is by no means an ideal or impersonal entity. He is mostly over 35 and under 50, has experienced war, marriage, and the responsibility of children, belongs in part to some kind of minority group, is male and not female, and shares most of Slatoff's general ways of thinking and feeling. His experience in the war does affect his feelings toward Jake and he cannot view Cohn as he might if he were the reading self of Lyndon B. Johnson, Henry Miller, Lord David Cecil, or Ernest Hemingway. Because I am a gardener of sorts I do not, as I read "April is the cruelest month," say merely, "How true. He's talking about plants," but I probably do think more about the rebirth of bulbs and plants than the average city apartment dweller. This reading self tends to overreact to certain kinds of moral and psychological situations—to authority questions and pain, for example—much as I do in life, but also recognizes this tendency and resists and watches it, but only up to a point.

This reading self, though more universalized than my fully defined personal self, is by no means an abstraction. It is still an individual self and feels like one, and the experiences it has are very much personal experiences.

If this sounds unduly obvious (and is what we usually mean by the term "educated reader") it is not so in most critical and theoretical discussion. Apart from occasional consideration of the problems of the modern reader confronting older works or the dilemma of a nonbeliever confronting doctrinaire religious works, scarcely ever does a critic even suggest that his reading or evaluation is in any way related to his personal qualities even in this generalized or universalized sense. And although we really know better, we have almost always talked and taught as though there were no middle ground between the impressionist and the definitionless theoretical or ideal reader. And we have supposed that the proper or true or best reading of a work would be that provided either by this theoretical reader or by a chameleon-like reader who became as nearly identical as possible with the consciousness which created and informed the novel. Or, of course, we have pretended that the work can have a "reading" without a reader.

If we were to acknowledge that all good readings are, in fact, performed by only partly depersonalized beings, and were to reckon with this fact in what we call criticism, or even to base criticism on this fact, we would, of course, run against problems (some of which I consider in my next chapter) that ideal readers and literary *objects* allow to remain in hiding. But we would also allow ourselves to get beyond disgracefully oversimple notions of the personal and the impersonal and of detachment and involvement; and we might, paradoxically, move closer to full objective truth about the works we read.

Chapter 3

The Divergence of Responses

THE RESPONSES of all but the most insane readers are to some degree guided and limited by the literary work they are reading. Even those for whom literature is largely a drug or gymnasium cannot help but pay some attention to the intention and movement of the work. And all responsible readers try very hard to respond in accord with what they take to be the intention or vision of the author and the work. They try as best they can both to understand and feel the point of view, attitudes, tone, mood, biases, and so forth which inform what they read. To do less than this is to disrespect the work and to cheat oneself of almost everything which makes good literature valuable.

Stated in such a way the reader's obligations seem clear enough. Like Henry James' ideal critic, he would seek to be "the real helper of the artist, a torch-bearing outrider, the interpreter, the brother . . . armed *cap-à pie* in curiosity and sympathy . . . to lend himself, to project himself and steep himself, to feel and feel till he understands . . . to be infinitely curious and incorrigibly patient, and yet plastic and inflammable and determinable." [1] In short, he would seek to shape and attune himself to the work as closely and completely as he could, to become, so to speak, the perfect instrument for sounding and resounding to it. Yet however necessary this ideal and however well it is sometimes achieved in practice, it is not sufficient and it rests upon surprisingly inadequate conceptions of the nature of readers, reading, and literary works themselves.

First of all, literary works, however firmly designed, can exert only limited and inexact control and guidance over even the most docile and sympathetic reader. No matter how carefully designed the rhetoric, how skillful the use of emphasis and subordination, how narrowly defined the attitudes or point of view, a work of any but the shortest and simplest sort must by its very nature leave its readers a great deal of freedom. Whole areas of response can scarcely be controlled at all, others provided with only the loosest limits.

I have spoken earlier of the wide range of uncontrollable individual differences on the sensory level alone, of the differences in the thresholds of response of our various senses, of the difference in the prominence of our senses in relation to one another. And I do not see how we can quarrel with Simon Lesser's assertion that "there is no necessary relationship between the amount of significance an image possesses for an author and its effect upon us.

[1] Henry James, *Essays in London and Elsewhere* (New York: Harper & Brothers, 1893), p. 264.

. . . Under the best of conditions I doubt if there is often an exact correspondence between the meaning an image possesses for author and reader. *Some* of the meanings the image had for the author will of course be communicated, but others may not be and still others may be added." [2] But even if we ignore questions of significance and meaning and ask merely how vividly or precisely we are to visualize a particular image, the work can provide only modest guidance. I am quite sure that some female students of mine who were offended by Marvell's "then worms shall try that long preserv'd virginity" were visualizing more specifically than the tone of the poem advises, and I am quite sure I ought better to control my picture of the narrator of "Annabel Lee" lying "down by the side" of his darling, his life, and his bride "In the sepulchre there by the sea— / In her tomb by the sounding sea." But in neither case can the work set anything like exact limits.

When it comes, of course, to metaphor and symbol, which are designed to provide richness rather than precision, the limits of response, of even entirely appropriate response, become much wider. And since literature does rely so heavily on images, metaphor, and symbol, this area of openness alone is substantial.

Nor can the work precisely govern the strength and intensity of many kinds of emotional response. George Eliot can instruct and persuade her reader to feel sympathy for Casaubon, and she can heighten that sympathy by making the reader think of him as a "lamed creature," but she cannot control with any degree of exactness the amount

[2] *Fiction and the Unconscious* (New York: Vintage Books, 1962), p. 159.

of sympathy which any given reader will feel, for this will depend on the intensity of his normal responses to suffering, his general attitude toward people like Casaubon, and numerous other aspects of his psyche which even he, let alone the author, cannot fully control. The violent divergence in responses to Shylock even among skillful and sophisticated readers is an extreme illustration of the range of response a work may allow, but it suggests something of the extent of the variation that any work may have to limit and the impossibility of any exact control. I suspect that the difficulty of governing degrees of pity and sympathy is peculiarly great for reasons I will discuss later, but the latitude we have for such feelings as amusement, scorn, terror, or affection cannot be much more closely circumscribed.

Perhaps least subject to control by either work or reader are certain fundamental differences in our general and almost instinctive feelings about order and disorder, restraint and freedom, roughness and smoothness, stillness and motion, directness and indirectness, feelings which affect our responses to the very form and texture of the work. Heroic couplets make some readers feel good—safe and comfortable; others have to learn to live with them, as with girdles or tight collars. Some breathe freely and expand as they encounter the rhythms of "Song of Myself." Others feel insecure. Some actively enjoy the delays and suspensions of a writer like Faulkner; others can barely abide them; still others are deeply ambivalent. Similarly we must vary greatly in our instinctive responses to various rhythms, tempos, tones, atmospheres, and narrative voices. I am speaking now only of virtually uncontrollable and unconscious orientations of our being, so to speak, areas which neither we nor the work can do much about. The variations are even greater in our attitudes, values, and beliefs—matters I will consider shortly.

Similarly uncontrollable by the work itself are various mental, emotional, and even physiological predispositions which can seriously affect our responses. Writers cannot control such things as the reader's momentary or habitual degree of dyspepsia or the degree of caution or distance with which he approaches all experience or his general degree of sympathy toward any particular modes of thought and feeling or whether he reads mainly for fun or mainly for duty; nor can they control changes in these predispositions which occur throughout whole ages or societies. A Donne poem gets read by a Dr. Johnson and a T. S. Eliot. Shelley can do nothing about some modern readers who, try as they will, can at best merely control their irritation toward him.

Nor can writers do very much about the general contrariness of humankind. As Kenneth Burke so brilliantly emphasizes in his essay "War, Response, and Contradiction," [3] humans do not respond in simple ways to stimuli and often react in ways that are or seem contradictory. He points out, for example, that a man is more likely to want to serve a cause if he is shown how painful and difficult such service is than if he is shown how glorious. Something similar is undoubtedly often true for responses to a variety of tones and attitudes governing literary works. We normally assume that a detached or ironic tone will

[3] *The Philosophy of Literary Form* (Baton Rouge: Louisiana State University Press, 1941), pp. 234–257.

induce a similar response in the reader and the same for highly involved and sympathetic tones. But this isn't necessarily the case. I think, for example, that I feel less detachment from Emma and Mr. Knightley than I do from Mellors and Lady Chatterley, yet surely Jane Austen is more cool and detached than D. H. Lawrence. And just as one may retreat icily when Dickens begins to slobber over a sympathetic character one may draw closer as a Nabokov or Mary McCarthy backs off impersonally in the face of suffering.

These things are obvious enough, though not often talked about or taken into account in criticism and teaching. Less obvious is the relatively limited exactitude with which works define the attitudes and values which are appropriate to them. I am not speaking now of clashes between author's and reader's attitudes, values, or beliefs, or of resistance to the author's views, which has received some excellent discussion by Wayne Booth and others and which I will turn to shortly, but merely of the thoroughness with which literature does communicate attitudes and value systems—does gratify the reader's need, as Wayne Booth puts it, "to know where, in the world of values, he stands—that is, to know where the author *wants* him to stand." [4] Every work provides some ground, some limits. No matter how much the work pretends to be photography or slices of life, it provides, if only by what is selected and omitted, something less than all possible viewpoints. At the other extreme, no work, no matter how simpleminded or polemical or bigoted, no matter how continually the author

[4] *The Rhetoric of Fiction* (Chicago: The University of Chicago Press, 1961), p. 73.

tells us directly, or indirectly, what to think and feel, can entirely define the attitudes to be applied at any given moment. We can be instructed to hiss the villain but not how loudly and how often. In short, no intention can fully comprehend or control all the complexities that a substantial literary work brings into being.

The majority of works provide some general guidelines and limits, and some very clear indications of attitude toward certain matters, but leave large areas to the reader's discretion. The areas may be as crucial and broad as those in works with unreliable narrators like Ford's *The Good Soldier* or Faulkner's *As I Lay Dying*, where the reader must continually, and with only the most subtle and ambiguous hints, make important decisions about the significance of actions and events, decisions upon which the whole meaning of the novel depends. They may be as circumscribed as in *Pilgrim's Progress* or Hemingway's *The Old Man and the Sea*, where the reader is required only to flesh out, so to speak, and to experience in the particular way that he experiences, the general attitudes he has been instructed and persuaded to apply. But whatever the limits, the reader must bring something of himself to bear. He cannot become merely a carbon copy of an authorial point of view, because not enough of the copy is written. He cannot passively undergo the author's experience of the work because the most the author can provide are guides and stimuli to the experience. He cannot undergo that experience merely by suspending his disbelief or usual state of consciousness. The reader simply cannot do what A. C. Bradley and so many others suggest he do if he wishes to possess the world of a poem fully: "Enter that world, conform to its laws, and ignore for the time the beliefs, aims, and particular conditions which belong to you in the other world of reality." [5] He can leave some of his idiosyncrasies behind, but he cannot even read and understand the poem unless he brings some of his intellectual and emotional possessions along. Only a "someone" can enter a world. Or as M. H. Abrams puts it: "Given a truly impassive reader, all his beliefs suspended or anesthetized, [a poet] would be as helpless, in his attempt to endow his work with interest and power, as though he had to write for an audience from Mars." [6] In a word, because literature counts on it, the reader must bring his own consciousness and experience to bear.

But how much of them? This, both in theory and practice, is the crucial question. To answer it, as even so astute a critic as I. A. Richards does, by saying in connection with personal memories that one brings to bear what is relevant and appropriate, is only to beg the question. To say one should bring to bear one's whole consciousness (as we shall see) still leaves the question unanswered.

Scholars and educational institutions and most critics seem to have accepted the notion that almost any amount of knowledge may be relevant to a literary work: knowledge about the social, political, and intellectual history of the period in which the work was written, knowledge about the sources of the work and the tradition of which

[5] A. C. Bradley, *Oxford Lectures on Poetry*, quoted in M. H. Abrams, "Belief and the Suspension of Disbelief," *Literature and Belief: English Institute Essays, 1957*, ed. M. H. Abrams (New York: Columbia University Press, 1958), p. 8.

[6] "Belief and the Suspension of Disbelief," *Literature and Belief*, p. 17.

it forms a part, knowledge about the development of the work itself, its germination, its revisions, its textual variants, knowledge about the life and experience of its author. Our curriculum structures, seminars, professional journals, teaching assignments, status hierarchies, and so forth all imply some such belief. Or to put it a little differently, we believe that any knowledge which will illuminate, enrich, or add to the dimensions of the work is relevant knowledge.

When it comes to the relevance of feelings, experiences, memories, attitudes, values, and beliefs, however, and the extent to which these are to be brought to bear, there is, with one exception, a curious silence—curious because perhaps the thing we most agree upon is that students and teachers alike must, above all, read responsively and with insight and awareness. The exception is the question of belief, enough of an exception to have occasioned substantial interest for many years and quite recently a symposium at the English Institute.[7] At this symposium and elsewhere, considerable attention has been given to the status of beliefs and dogma in literary works and to the question how and to what extent works in which such elements bulk large can be appreciated by readers who do not share those beliefs or have opposed ones. Can a Protestant, for example, properly experience *The Divine Comedy* or an atheist *Paradise Lost?* Particularly valuable in this discussion, it

[7] The papers read at the symposium are collected under the title *Literature and Belief* in the volume cited above. The volume also contains a selected bibliography and a brief summary by M. H. Abrams of the general lines of argument over the years (pp. 1–13).

seems to me, is M. H. Abrams' general assertion that "our experience in reading serious literature, when uninhibited by theoretical prepossessions, engages the whole mind, including the complex of common sense and moral beliefs and values deriving from our experience in this world," [8] and his recognition that our beliefs "subsist less in propositional form than in the form of unverbalized attitudes, propensities, sentiments, and dispositions; but they stand ready to precipitate into assertions the moment they are radically challenged, whether in the ordinary course of living or in that part of living we call reading poetry." [9] I would wish to add, however, that these unverbalized attitudes and propensities may express themselves as feelings, reservations, observations, even when not radically challenged but merely touched in some way.

Also valuable, I think, is W. J. Ong's distinction between "belief that" and "belief in." Surely he is right that much of our willingness to go along with ideas and attitudes we do not share is due to our "belief in" the author or narrator—our belief that, despite certain disagreements, he will say something worthy of our assent or contemplation.[10] I do not think, however, that this willingness to go along with is as full or single a thing as Father Ong implies, nor can I quite accept his view that artistic communication has a curiously one-way nature and that no real dialogue takes place.[11] In the reader's consciousness a

[8] *Ibid.*, p. 11.
[9] *Ibid.*, p. 16.
[10] "Voice as Summons for Belief, *Literature and Belief*, pp. 101–104.
[11] *Ibid.*, p. 102.

dialogue does take place, and not merely a dialogue but a much fuller set of relations. Mark Twain may not be able to hear my grumbling and cries of anger as I read the later sections of *Huckleberry Finn*, but my psyche behaves as though he could.

Wayne Booth's discussion of "The Role of Belief" [12] is also important and illuminating. I think he overestimates the extent to which a reader must and can subordinate his mind and heart to the book and must become, so to speak, a second self which corresponds to the "implied" or "second self" of the author, but he is more aware than most of the difficulties this subordination may entail. As he says, "We may exhort ourselves to read tolerantly, we may quote Coleridge on the willing suspension of disbelief until we think ourselves totally suspended in a relativistic universe, and still we will find many books which postulate readers we refuse to become, books that depend on 'beliefs' or 'attitudes' . . . which we cannot adopt even hypothetically as our own" (p. 138). He asserts also that "one of our most common reading experiences is, in fact, the discovery on reflection that we have allowed ourselves to become a 'mock reader' whom we *cannot* respect, that the beliefs which we were temporarily manipulated into accepting cannot be defended in the light of day" (p. 139). I have been arguing and hope to show that as we read we struggle more than he suggests against this sort of self-betrayal.

This discussion of "belief" has been valuable in many ways, but almost all of it focuses only on major conflicts or discrepancies between beliefs and implies that such

[12] *The Rhetoric of Fiction*, pp. 137–144.

conflicts are special cases or deviations from a norm of nearly complete harmony between author and reader. I would argue that such conflicts are merely extreme forms of a condition that obtains to one degree or another in all our literary experiences and that a complete correspondence of attitudes is not a norm but another extreme, one which may, in fact, interfere with a judicious or even adequate response as much as a violent opposition of values. We could all name some works which we view with special glasses because their attitudes, explicit or implicit, so closely resemble our own that they gain not merely our assent but our applause and admiration. Our usual experience, it seems to me, involves a curiously complex set of adjustments and maladjustments between our own views and ways of feeling and those which inform the work, a set of adjustments much more like those in a successful marriage than in, say, a dream or brainwashing. It is an experience involving minor irritations, questions, skepticisms, and reservations of all sorts. As in any relation that is not completely harmonious, we will sometimes defer to the author, sometimes accept things for the sake of the argument, sometimes entertain notions indulgently and give the benefit of the doubt, sometimes suspend judgment temporarily, sometimes mutter or grumble or give a tolerant smile, sometimes view with distaste, suspicion, alarm, or dismay, sometimes revise an impression eagerly, sometimes begrudgingly, sometimes rise fiercely up in arms, sometimes wonder anxiously where the author stands, and so on. The critical discussion of the matter so far seems to envision only two sorts of marriages—blissful and miserable.

Nor has the discussion of belief suggested anything like the full dimensions of the question how much the reader is to bring to bear, for, as I have already indicated, much more than beliefs or even attitudes is involved. Nor has the discussion indicated anything like the range and kinds of maladjustment or tension that may occur between the reader and the work.

One major class of maladjustments might be termed *unaccommodated awareness,* awareness which is not clearly excluded by the work, but which pulls against what one takes to be the intention of the work or the authorial point of view. Few readers and writers are in such close harmony that a reading can occur without at least some minor tensions of this sort. One may, for example, while reading *Tom Jones,* essentially go along with the tone and attitudes that govern the work and yet be troubled by qualities of blindness, pride, and stupidity in Squire All-worthy that make one at least smile at his name and at Fielding's apparently uncritical view of him. (No one else is fooled by Thwackum, Square or Blifil.) And one may be jarred out of harmony with the final pages of the book by an awareness that Squire Western is bringing about the desired end through the same kind of blind ruthlessness which earlier led to so much pain and difficulty. In this, as in other of the examples to follow, one may decide that the author intends these awarenesses or shares them, but one experiences at the very last a nagging uncertainty. In *The Sun Also Rises,* one may feel that in the course of celebrating his stoicism Jake Barnes finds too many ways to remind us how much he is suffering. Or even if one thinks, as I do much of the time, that *Middle-*

71

march is the greatest English novel, one may not be able
to share fully the author's view of Will Ladislaw or Mary
Garth. The most devoted admirers of Jane Austen may
not be able to avoid becoming more aware of the narrator
than of Emma and Mr. Knightley at the moment when,
flustered by her own love scene, Jane Austen retreats
wildly and gives Emma's answer to Mr. Knightley in the
form of "What did she?—Just what she ought, of course.
A lady always does." And an only slightly less devout
Austenite might feel that by devoting more than half the
final paragraph of *Emma* to a last flurry of jabs at Mrs.
Elton, Miss Austen had become nearly as bitchy as her
victim. It is difficult, in fact, to think of a work of any
substantial length in which one does not experience at
some point either some sense of discrepancy between one's
own and the author's evaluation of someone or something,
or some tone or emphasis which one cannot fully share, or
some unaccommodated sense that the author has been
pompous or immature, or biased or sentimental or callous or
glib or unduly cautious or merely uncertain. At the very
least there will be occasions when we wonder whether our
perceptions are in accord with those of the author, whether
they are accommodated. We will have some such questions
in almost any work where the narrator is a character or
where the point of view is that of a single character, in a
work, that is, where we must decide whether particular
moral or intellectual limitations of the character are meant
to be noticed or not and are meant to determine our view
of him. Does Conrad see that Marlow sometimes unwit-
tingly closes his eyes to darkness or flees from involvement? Does Hemingway recognize Jake's thinly disguised

pleas for our pity? Does Joyce recognize certain of Stephen's pretensions? Does Richardson share any of our amusement or annoyance at Pamela's opportunism? Whether we finally answer such questions or merely table them, the asking and uncertainty become part of our experience of the work. That they do so doesn't necessarily mean that we are superior to the author, but merely that the author has exposed himself and we have not.

I have been talking so far about relatively minor and momentary tensions between the work and the reader, but in many instances they are much more deep and far-reaching. The most serious maladjustments arise when the reader feels that a writer has missed the crucial themes, implications, or complexities of his own work, or fails completely to see through the posturings of his hero, or is generally simple-minded or immature. This relation occurs chiefly when one is reading the work of young students, unpublished manuscripts, autobiographical first novels, or certain sorts of mass circulation fiction. But it may arise in only slightly less extreme form with works of greater merit like Wolfe's *Look Homeward, Angel,* Hemingway's *Across the River and into the Trees,* and Mailer's *An American Dream.* For some readers, at least, Richardson's *Pamela,* Dickens' *Bleak House,* and Lawrence's *Lady Chatterley's Lover* might also fall into this category, as might many romantic poems. That is, the reader may feel not only that there is a clash between his own and the author's values and perceptions, but that the author has failed to see important problems and qualities that his own work or major character dramatizes, qualities which he could and should have seen.

Only slightly less serious are those instances where the reader finds himself continually aware of qualities in the narrator or author which he finds unattractive or offensive. I may learn to live with the smugness of Thackeray, Meredith, or James Gould Cozzens, but my awareness of that smugness is an inevitable part of my experience of their works. It is not merely that the awareness provides a kind of counterpoint or background of annoyance and wariness or adds to my general distance from the work; it colors and complicates most of my moment-to-moment responses. One might react similarly to the self-indulgent tone of Jack Kerouac, the sadism of Mickey Spillane, the prurience of a Grace Metalious or Irving Wallace, or the sentimentality of a Louis Bromfield or Anne Morrow Lindbergh.

Where one becomes unduly aware of the author for stylistic rather than moral reasons the tension is less acute but nevertheless a maladjustment insofar as the awareness is unaccommodated or unintended by the work. I rather like the lumbering presence of Dreiser which stands beside Sister Carrie and sometimes gets in front of her, but I know as I read that he doesn't know he is there. One's awareness of the presence of a Faulkner or James is something else again. If one is put off by their style or mannerisms a maladjustment will occur and one's experience of the work will be affected, but there is no ironic relation or unaccommodated perception because the authors intend and want to be noticed.

A fairly large number of works engender unaccommodated perceptions by what may be called their countercurrents, that is some element in the work—of structure, point of view, tone, attitude, pattern, or meaning—which runs against the main drift of the work. If, for example, either on one's own or through reading some critic, one becomes aware of the minor motif in *Hamlet* which associates Hamlet with sickness and Claudius with health, or feels the attractiveness of Satan in *Paradise Lost*, or begins to worry whether or not Emma Woodhouse has really learned anything, what is one to do with such awarenesses? One can let C. S. Lewis persuade one that *Paradise Lost* will not really allow Blake's or Shelley's readings of it, but there is enough Blake and Shelley in the make-up of most of us to prevent us from a full accommodation to the work. In each of these instances and many others our experience may include a set of mental and emotional awarenesses which we cannot and ought not simply banish and which give that experience a discordant quality.

Apart from those maladjustments which are more or less directly generated by elements in the works themselves are those which come about because readers are complex human beings and simply cannot at will shut off certain portions of their consciousness once they have become engaged in an activity which calls their minds and emotions into serious activity. What concerns me here is not so much particular ideas or beliefs which openly and definably oppose those of the author or work and which for that reason are relatively easy to manage and talk about, but rather a host of less formulated attitudes, values, feelings, and intellectual and temperamental biases which make one's relation to the work something less than fully harmonious.

One source of such discord is the inevitable temporal gap between the modern reader and an older work. No matter how universal or timeless the work, no matter how much the reader trains himself to become a part of the audience for whom the work was originally written, social, political, and literary history has intervened and provided the reader with conscious and unconscious perspectives which neither he nor the work can obliterate. These perspectives will sometimes take such obvious forms as nostalgia or impatience; they may include conscious thoughts and feelings about a later author or style, a later society or war, a later philosophic or psychological theory; they may be no more than a dim awareness that time and distance have, in fact, intervened.

Another source of such discord may be the conscious or unconscious purpose for which one is reading. The student who is reading for an exam or the scholar who is reading with a practical or psychological need to order or formulate his experience cannot be entirely in tune with a work like *Leaves of Grass* which keeps telling him again and again that the work is to be felt rather than understood and that "No shutter'd room or school can commune with me,/ But roughs and little children better than they." The reader who is yearning for hope or security will be in an uneasy relation with a writer like Donne or Faulkner who delights in uncertainty and paradox. Those who read fiction largely out of an interest in the way man copes in the public world of social actions and manners are likely to read Kafka and Beckett with some uneasiness. These are illustrations of extreme cross-purposes. Our knowledge of the general human talent for achieving conditions of cross-purpose should suggest the extent to which it is true of reading.

A somewhat similar sort of maladjustment may come about because of some basic conflict or difference of interest between author and reader. I am awed and dazzled by Joyce and Nabokov, for example, and I read their works with pleasure, excitement, and, I like to think, understanding. At the same time, however, I experience a tension and discomfort as I am forced to recognize again and again that while my deepest concern has been with the psychological and ethical relations they have created, their own deepest fascination has been with language. Those who are most fully in accord with the interests of Joyce and Nabokov will probably experience something of a similar sort as they read, say, *Middlemarch* or *An American Tragedy*. Similar sorts of differences between reader and author can exist with respect to their relative interest in the individual as against the group, in ethics as against metaphysics, in morals as against aesthetics, and so on. And this is to say nothing of the maladjustments which occur with readers whose dominant approaches to all experience are Marxist, Thoreauvian, psychoanalytic, devoutly Christian, or nihilistic. Even when there is no major divergence of interest or attitude there may well be minor tensions and dislocations if the reader has even a piece of his mind that belongs to Marx, Thoreau, D. H. Lawrence, St. Thomas, or De Sade. Good readers with one or another of these general interests or biases will try to distinguish between those value judgments and systems which lie within the general ken of the work and those outside it. And they will not project their biases into the work itself and convert, say, Shakespeare into an Existentialist. But their unaccommodated perceptions will still be part of their experience. Only a politician or chameleon can alter his coloring sufficiently to blend equally well with, say, Dostoevsky and James, Melville and Trollope, Blake and Pope, Dickens and Virginia Woolf, Meredith and George Eliot. My point here, let me try to be perfectly clear, is not that tastes vary or that readers will evaluate works in relation to their own interests or temperaments but that these variations lead to differing relations between readers and works and differing sorts of experiences and render foolish the notion of an ideal or uniform harmony between reader and work.

I have not answered, of course, either in general or in specific terms the question I asked earlier about how much the reader should bring to bear. I hope I have shown that part of the process of reading, itself, is a way of asking the question. One will, if one is a good reader, bring to bear all the knowledge and experience one has which will aid the work in fulfilling its intentions, and one will exclude as best one can knowledges, experiences, and associations which are clearly inappropriate, but if one is reading as a human being one will also inevitably bring to bear attitudes, feelings, vantage points, and perceptions which the work has not called for. One will wonder and speculate about their relevance and appropriateness and in so doing may come to feel some degree of tension between oneself and the work. But that seems to me a fine price to pay in order to be a real rather than ideal reader.

For reasons which I hope will be clear later, I have reserved until now, for separate and extended discussion, what seems to me the most crucial area of adjustment and maladjustment between reader and work. It can best be approached, I think, through *Middlemarch*. At the beginning of Chapter 20 we discover that Dorothea is sobbing. With a detached but sympathetic tone George Eliot goes on to analyze at some length the reason for her tears and then writes:

Nor can I suppose that when Mrs. Casaubon is discovered in a fit of weeping six weeks after her wedding, the situation will be regarded as tragic. Some discouragement, some faintness of heart at the real new future which replaces the imaginary, is not unusual, and we do not expect people to be deeply moved by what is not unusual. That element of tragedy which lies in the very fact of frequency, has not yet wrought itself into the coarse emotion of mankind; and perhaps our frames could hardly bear much of it. If we had a keen vision and feeling of all ordinary human life, it would be like hearing the grass grow and the squirrel's heart beat, and we should die of that roar which lies on the other side of silence. As it is, the quickest of us walk about well wadded with stupidity.[13]

We may note first that the passage allows the reader a rather wide range of response. The tone, as well as the content of the entire description, suggests that the reader view Dorothea with a degree of sympathy but that he need not be "deeply moved," need not regard her condition in any way as tragic. At the same time George Eliot has indicated that there is an element of tragedy in the situation (which she can perceive), which might move us deeply if our emotion were less coarse and we had a keen enough vision and feeling and if we were not so "well

[13] George Eliot, *Middlemarch* (Boston: Houghton Mifflin Company, 1956), p. 144. Subsequent references will be provided in the text.

wadded with stupidity." In this way she has not only per-
mitted but encouraged us to try to respond with more
sympathy, anguish, and involvement than her own tone
has directed. And despite her warning that too keen a
vision, too much compassion, would be unbearable, might
even destroy us, she has both in the passage and in the
book as a whole urged us to become less "wadded," or,
to draw from a later section of the book, to resist, as Bul-
strode did not, the "padding [of] the moral sensibility" (p.
451).

Much of *Middlemarch* is an attempt to cut through that
wadding or padding on her characters and readers, an effort to make heard that roar behind the silence. Thus she
labors to make us hear the pain even of the dried-up Casaubon and the frivolous Rosamond, and one of the most
powerful scenes in the book (and perhaps in any book)
shows the pain and rewards that come when one does
allow oneself to hear and the terrible danger if one doesn't.
Dorothea has been deeply hurt and angered by Casaubon's
refusal to accept her presence and concern after he learns
that he might die suddenly, and she wants to hurt him.
But she fights her anger by remembering how much he
must have suffered earlier that day.

It cost her a litany of pictured sorrows and of silent cries that
she might be the mercy for those sorrows—but the resolved
submission did come; and when the house was still, and she
knew that it was near the time when Mr. Casaubon habitually
went to rest, she opened her door gently and stood outside
in the darkness waiting for his coming upstairs with a light
in his hand. If he did not come soon she thought that she
would go down and even risk incurring another pang. She
would never again expect anything else. But she did hear the

library door open, and slowly the light advanced up the staircase without noise from the footsteps on the carpet. When her husband stood opposite to her, she saw that his face was more haggard. He started slightly on seeing her, and she looked up at him beseechingly, without speaking.

"Dorothea!" he said, with a gentle surprise in his tone. "Were you waiting for me?"

"Yes, I did not like to disturb you."

"Come, my dear, come. You are young, and need not to extend your life by watching."

When the kind quiet melancholy of that speech fell on Dorothea's ears, she felt something like the thankfulness that might well up in us if we had narrowly escaped hurting a lamed creature. She put her hand into her husband's, and they went along the broad corridor together. (Pp. 313–314.)

Here both content and tone persuade us toward maximum compassion for both characters, and lest our wadding still deafen us, George Eliot makes a final effort to penetrate by equating Dorothea's feeling with the thankfulness not she but *we* would have felt had we narrowly escaped hurting a lamed creature. We know by this time in *Middlemarch* and even more certainly after this passage that even if George Eliot had not chosen to spell out Dorothea's feeling of thankfulness or to encourage us to see Casaubon as a lamed creature, we had the right and even the obligation ourselves to provide those awarenesses and the feelings that attach to them. We know that as readers we are to bring to bear our maximum compassion and moral awareness.

There will be some readers with permanent or temporary ideas, attitudes, or emotional conditions which prevent them from sharing these views which George Eliot has been encouraging and who will experience the sort of malaccommodation or discordance I have spoken of earlier. But I am not much concerned with such responses because I do not believe many readers who care about literature would feel so and because I would see such readers as afflicted not so much with unaccommodated awareness as with unduly thick moral padding or wadding.

What I want to bring forward from this illustration are the observations that few writers direct and control our moral sensibilities as clearly as George Eliot does and that readers and writers vary greatly in the thickness of their wadding and in their receptivity to that roar on the other side of silence. Or to put it less moralistically, they vary greatly in the ease with which other awarenesses and feelings of theirs will be penetrated or overthrown by the silent sound of pain. Or to put it another way, we vary greatly in the degree to which we are willing or able to achieve points of view or aesthetic distances from which the sound of pain is inaudible. Or to put it still another way, we vary in our willingness to ignore the victim's point of view.

Very few readers are willing or able to share the view and distance which controls Vittorio Mussolini's vision when he writes that the explosion of a bomb in the midst of a group of Ethiopian horsemen was like a rose bursting into bloom, and most amusing.[14] However thickly wadded,

[14] *Voli Sulle Ambe* (Firenze: G. C. Sansoni, editore, 1937), pp. 47–48. The passage reads: "Ho ancora in mente l'effetto di un gruppetto di Galla, caracollanti dietro ad uno vestito di nero, sbocciare, come una rosa, essendogli piombato in mezzo qualche tubo della mia gelatiera. Era molto divertente e si colpivano bene anche stando relativamente alti, data l'ampiezza del terreno che occupavano questi armati."

most of us, despite the author's determined deafness, cannot help but hear the cries of pain, cannot help but entertain the victims' point of view. And most of us would be disturbed by a reader who could not do so. We would be similarly dismayed by a reader who was amused at or indifferent to the deaths of Lear and Cordelia even if that reader were sophisticated enough to argue that his was the superior vantage point of the gods, who like wanton boys with flies, kill us for their sport.

A somewhat smaller but still large number of us are deeply at odds with the latter sections of *Huckleberry Finn* not so much for aesthetic reasons as because we cannot share Twain's amusement as he recounts the elaborate games by which Tom and Huck pretend to be liberating the chained and terrified Jim, who in fact is already free. To enjoy the fun we must view Jim as a one-dimensional comic figure, block all awareness of the anguish he is experiencing, and resist all temptation to see the events from Jim's point of view. Twain, in these sections, does everything he can to help us to achieve this.

But earlier in the book Twain himself has powerfully and brilliantly demonstrated to both Huck and the reader the ugliness and falsity of such a view. It is just that view which has enabled Huck to tease Jim by pretending that Jim had only dreamed that Huck was lost. And it is that wadded view which Twain so effectively demolishes through Jim's eloquent revelation of his pain and point of view:

"Oh, well, that's all interpreted well enough, as far as it goes, Jim," I says; "but what does *these* things stand for?"

It was the leaves and rubbish on the raft, and the smashed oar. You could see them first rate, now.

Jim looked at the trash, and then looked at me, and back at the trash again. He had got the dream fixed so strong in his head that he couldn't seem to shake it lose and get the facts back into its place again, right away. But when he did get the thing straightened around, he looked at me steady, without ever smiling, and says:

"What do dey stan' for? I's gwyne to tell you. When I got all wore out wid work, en wid de callin' for you, en went to sleep, my heart wuz mos' broke bekase you wuz los', en I didn' k'yer no mo' what become er me en de raf'. En when I wake up en fine you back agin', all safe en soun', de tears come en I could a got down on my knees en kiss' yo' foot I's so thankful. En all you wuz thinkin' 'bout wuz how you could make a fool uv ole Jim wid a lie. Dat truck dah is *trash;* en trash is what people is dat puts dirt on de head er dey fren's en makes 'em ashamed." [15]

Huck, we remember, is sufficiently penetrated by that "roar" to do what he never believed he could do: "It was fifteen minutes before I could work myself up to go and humble myself to a nigger—but I done it, and I warn't ever sorry for it afterwards, neither" (p. 121).

Most readers retain enough memory of this and other scenes which emphasize Jim's humanity to spoil the later comedy. It is not merely that they recognize intellectually that they are being asked to take on the sort of perspective or lack of it that led to Huck's lesson on the raft, but that they have been taught by the book itself to hear the cries of what look like comic figures.

Let us suppose, however, that Twain had not given Jim his say on the raft and had done little or nothing any-

[15] *The Adventures of Huckleberry Finn* (New York: Webster and Co., 1885), p. 121.

where in the book to encourage us to see and feel Jim as human. Suppose the tone and point of view had been consistently that of the later sections. If the reader then brought to bear those awarenesses which spoil the fun, he might appear from some vantage points a naïve reader and from others a stuffy moralist and from still others an unpleasant bleeding heart. Yet by not bringing them to bear he would be accepting a wadded condition that, in fact, even Huck and Twain, on some occasions at least, found intolerable and which we know is related to the deafness to the cries on slave ships and in the black hovels and ghettos ever since. I trust it is clear that this is not merely an idle speculation about a book which was never written, for the world is full of literary and other works whose points of view can be fully shared only if we withhold the kind of awarenesses Huck gains on the raft, only if we remain temporarily deaf to the silent cries and blind to the victim's point of view. One need not have a quivering moral sensibility to resist or refuse to share the vision behind many of the sadistic animated cartoons, the acceptance of whose atrocities we can manage only by studiously forgetting every single bit of one's knowledge about what it would be like for a cat really to be set on fire or run over by a steamroller. And one need not be immune to the joys of the pratfall or deny the validity of all comic vision to be a little uneasy about the responses called for by, say, some Restoration comedies or some novels by George Meredith or Mary McCarthy.

But to continue more gradually, one might move from *Huckleberry Finn* to a work which has troubled a somewhat smaller but still sizable segment of responders, *The*

Merchant of Venice. Here the entire problem is complicated by the fact that Shylock is a Jew and that we are post-Buchenwald readers. But leaving that aside for the moment, we may still have difficulty adjusting to the state of mind and feeling toward Shylock which are required by the latter parts of the play. Again, as in *Huckleberry Finn*, we have witnessed an eloquent plea which encourages us to share Shylock's point of view, which reminds us that even he can bleed and cry out in pain as we do. Even if we see his rhetoric merely as one additional proof of his cunning we are forced to assent to the truth of what he says. If we retain these awarenesses in the later scenes where we are to delight in his torment we will be out of adjustment with the play, which no longer accommodates such awarenesses. Again, as in *Huckleberry Finn*, had those awarenesses never been stimulated by the work itself, the viewer or reader who experienced them nevertheless might appear naïve or oversensitive. Yet by not bringing them to bear he would be failing to hear a "roar" which could be voiced in 1596 and for a moment at least be permitting himself to wear the kind of padding which could become thick enough to muffle or absorb the roar within the concentration camps and crematoriums.

But where can we stop what is beginning to look like an argument in favor of our standing always at full sober moral attention? If Casaubon is a lamed creature worthy of our compassion, what about Malvolio? Might there be those who resist sharing in the fun as he is mocked and tormented? We do after all, witness his misery in the dark room and hear him plead for help, and Olivia herself says,

"He hath been notoriously abus'd." I have known reasonably well wadded intelligent readers who have heard too much pain in such varied works as Nabokov's *Lolita,* Thurber's "A Couple of Hamburgers," Dorothy Parker's "I Live on Your Visits," Edith Wharton's "Roman Fever," and Faulkner's "Spotted Horses" to be able to share the author's degree of humor or detachment.

Whatever one decides about the natural or proper limits of sympathy it is clear that readers will vary greatly in their responses to human suffering and that these variations will put readers in very different states of adjustment to any particular work. And since fiction and drama depend so much for their meaning and total impact on such responses these variations will seriously affect the reader's experience and understanding of the work as a whole. It is clear also that these variations have moral relations and consequences which make them more than mere differences in point of view. To George Eliot, at least, the variation is in degree of padding and deafness.

We need not look at it so, of course, and insofar as I am concerned with adjustments between readers and books I should give equal space to the maladjustments which arise because the reader has a view of life which makes the compassion or moral earnestness of a particular writer seem inadequate or absurd. Certainly there are widely held and valid perspectives which cannot help but view any individual roar against the backdrop of eternity or history or the three and a half billion other human denizens of this globe and which find any undue fuss about one human fate amusing or unbecoming. And there is a view from which man's talent for attaching so much importance to his actions and experiences is what makes him most pretentious and absurd.

One need have scarcely any such perspective at all to find silly or amusing a large number of adolescent works in which the author assumes that everything which happens to his hero—first kiss, choice of college, first philosophic reflections, first experience of death, first love-making—is of cosmic importance. And one need not share much of the cosmic or comic perspective to be out of accord with certain portions of Thomas Wolfe, D. H. Lawrence, or Hemingway. Nor need one be hardhearted to resist the point of view which dominates in *Silas Marner* or even *Adam Bede*. Many readers whose detachment is still far short of that, say, of the narrator of *The Egoist* are more put off by the moral and philosophic pretensions of *Moby-Dick*, "Heart of Darkness," and even *Middlemarch* than they are moved by the human predicaments rendered in them. A relatively small number, I suppose, of those who care for good literature are so intellectually and emotionally persuaded of man's insignificance and absurdity that they must remain seriously out of accord with the tone and vision that control a *King Lear* or *Oedipus Rex*. But surely there must be degrees of accord, and surely there are times at which almost anyone may find it difficult to be persuaded that any experience of this human animal is worth more than a grimace or smile. If most animated cartoons could not survive the intrusion of a real cry or flow of blood, it is also true that all but the very greatest tragedies could not survive a certain kind of laughter and have lent themselves quite easily to parody. Regardless of instructions, individual temperaments and individual moods will confront the work of art with their own proclivities toward tears or laughter.

Of course, these two directions of vision and feeling are not so diametrically opposed as I seem to suggest. One can be amused by pretension and be compassionate toward human suffering; one can feel the absurdity of all human endeavor and feel the pathos of the endeavor itself; one can detest sentimentality and hate cruelty.

I should remember, also, that the view of man as comic can lead sometimes to a gentleness, tolerance, and flexibility of spirit that are humane and compassionate and that too great a sensitivity to pain and injustice sometimes breeds joyless fanaticisms more cruel and bloody than the injustices they bleed for. I should also pay some heed to C. S. Lewis's observation that "for about a hundred years we have so concentrated on one of the virtues—'kindness' or mercy—that most of us do not feel anything except kindness to be really good or anything but cruelty to be really bad. Such lopsided ethical developments are not uncommon, and other ages too have had their pet virtues and curious insensibilities." [16]

Despite these observations, there are crucial respects in which the two directions of vision and feeling are opposed and there are good reasons for arguing the superiority of compassion to detachment—matters I shall wish to pursue later. I have introduced a moral bias here in order to indicate that maladjustments and tensions between readers and works of art may involve something even more important

[16] Quoted from *The Problem of Pain* in Robert Liddell, *A Treatise on the Novel* (London: Jonathan Cape, 1947), pp. 60–61.

than divergent temperaments, attitudes, and beliefs and that an answer to the question how much a reader is to bring to bear may require fundamental moral and ethical assumptions and decisions. For a reader simply to share, while reading, the values and vision of the work would often require not only a suspension of disbelief but a suspension of moral judgment. I don't believe that readers actually do this except in a very special and partial way and that if they did achieve such a total suspension they wouldn't be able to understand most of what they read.

At this point it would look as though the texts themselves were in great jeopardy. They are. The moment we subject them to real rather than theoretical readers, they enter the actual world of human confrontations in which everything is in jeopardy. At the same time nothing I have said argues against the reader's obligation to try with all his resources to understand and feel the point of view, vision, and meanings of the work itself. Nor need such a pursuit be urged on the grounds of objectivity alone, for any morality which requires respect for the uniqueness and otherness of things outside the self requires that same respect be extended to works of art. What I am saying is that real respect requires not a suspension or withholding of the self and its full awarenesses but an exercise and offering of them. Obviously more needs to be said about this, and I will return to it, but we need first to look at two aspects of the reader's experience which complicate matters still further.

Chapter 4

The Presence
of Narrators

A<small>N IMPORTANT</small> part of our experience of almost any literary work is the sense that we are being talked to by someone. This human presence in the work, I believe, accounts for much of our pleasure in reading and for much of the value we attach to it. Our response to this presence, moreover, may greatly affect our taste for particular writers and works and our evaluation of them, just as qualities of the teller affect our response to any communication. Our very decision that a group of words are worth attending to is in part a decision that the teller is worth listening to.

A rough measure of the importance of this human presence is the dissatisfaction of most readers when it is absent or notably minimal. I say "most" rather than all because a certain number of readers, and writers and artists as well, have been so deeply conditioned to view the work of art as autonomous—as a mere set of internal relations—that they no longer seem to care whether those relations are accidental or not and perhaps no longer even notice the difference, though I doubt it. The majority of readers, however, want the sense not merely of a human hand behind the work but of a human consciousness informing it, the feeling that they are attending to an experience rather than a mere arrangement.[1]

> To belch yet not to boast,
>   that is the hug,
>
> The high lullaby's bay
>   discretely crushes the bug.
>
> Your science was so
>   minute and hilly;
>
> Yes I am not the jade organ's
>   leather programer's recipe.
>
> As she is squealing above the cheroot,
>   these obscure toilets shall squat.
>
> Moreover, on account of hunger,
>   the room was hot.[2]

This "poem" was written by a data-processing machine. It contains some provocative combinations of words and sounds. One might wish to dwell for a moment on the "high lullaby's bay" which "discretely crushes the bug" and ponder the implications of the "minute and hilly" science. One might even discover in the poem a certain am-

[1] See note 1, page 9.
[2] Wilbur Cross, "Machine Miltons," *The New York Times Magazine*, December 4, 1966, p. 64; © 1966 by the New York Times Company. Reprinted by permission.

bivalence on the machine's part as it says, "Yes I am not the . . . programer's recipe." But surely only another machine or a designer of such machines would find the poem worth much attention. It is not enough to explain this by saying that the poem lacks overall coherence or a consistent tone. What it lacks is that combination of a large number of qualities, many very minute and subtle, which convey the sense that a human consciousness has been at work. One can imagine, of course, and there will probably be developed much more skillful machines, ones that might produce poems which could not easily be distinguished from human productions, but this is merely to say that these machines will have received a fuller infusion of human qualities and will produce a better imitation of the work of a human consciousness. We might say that the poem above was created by giving to a machine some human qualities and that the poem interests us only to the extent that it does reflect the work of a human consciousness.

As yet we have few productions of machines trying to act like men; most insufficiently human creations are the products of men trying to act like machines, and our dissatisfaction with these is indicated by the heavily pejorative connotation of the label "mechanical" which we often give to them. Exercises are of limited interest in part because we recognize that we are encountering not so much a mind using a literary form to explore or give shape to an experience as a mind deliberately curtailing its activity in order to produce a form or to develop a skill. We recognize, I think, that a work is an exercise less by the qualities it does possess than by those it doesn't. Our interest in acrostic and shaped poems and other sorts of ingenious fabrication is limited for much the same reason. We are witnessing a task rather than an experience, a mind reduced to an instrument for problem solving. Even the most brilliant activity of this sort—the *tour de force*—compels admiration rather than a full response. The very term announces our recognition that we have encountered something less than a human expression.

I don't mean to erect here any simple opposition between the formal and the human or to suggest that our sense of the author is fullest when he has accepted the fewest restrictions, that Allen Ginsberg, say, provides more sense of a human presence than Pope. Indeed, it is as human to express oneself through manners and conventions as it is to chant and cry out. The distinction I am making at the moment is between a mind working within limits and a mind intent on doing a technical job. In one case we sense a mind, in the other a motive.

When we read a story or poem which has clearly been written in terms of a formula we are disappointed not because we object to formulas per se but because we feel we have been offered only an organization of materials. Much the same is true of our response to works we call academic or routine or wooden, or lifeless or imitative, whatever the particular epithets we choose. We are saying not merely that the works lack certain qualities we find desirable for their own sake but that we miss the sense of a living consciousness informing the work. Originality is not simply a novel arrangement of materials—that can be accomplished by removing or transposing the second and fourth words of every sentence—but evidence that a mind has been at work.

A somewhat more curious measure of the importance of our sense of an authorial presence is our irritation when we feel we have been fooled, when we discover some piece of evidence that the teller was less present than we had felt he was. If, for example, as happens frequently to editors of magazines and teachers of writing, one reads what seems to be a serious presentation of some human predicament and then discovers that it was all fabricated to lead up to a trick ending, one feels not merely that the ending is unsatisfactory or inappropriate; one feels cheated, betrayed. What is betrayed is one's trust that one was in communication with a mind fully attending to and caring about what it was saying. The experience is not unlike the discovery that something one has read was plagiarized. In both cases what one thought was the revelation of a mind again becomes merely the encounter with a motive. To a lesser degree one has this same sense of betrayal when a particularly inappropriate metaphor or descriptive inaccuracy reveals that the writer was paying less attention to his material than one had thought. And perhaps our annoyance rather than simple boredom with clichés in a work results from a similar recognition, a similar feeling of deprivation. Our concern with establishing correct texts and our uneasiness about translations may be less a quest for accuracy than a need to feel that we are in touch with the product of a single mind.

So far I have been talking only about our response to the presence or absence of some human mind, our concern that *someone* be talking to us, rather than of our response to any particular mind or any particular qualities of that mind. Obviously if little or no activity of mind of any sort is present there can be few individual qualities revealed. Just as obviously, the presence of individual qualities will provide a sense that some consciousness is present. But I am suggesting that even apart from our sense of such individualities, we respond to the presence and activity of human consciousness in a work. We do more than recognize that the work has been produced by another human creature, we feel the humanness of the activity, feel that we are experiencing not merely a creation or handiwork but a man's creation and handiwork—art rather than scenery. Beyond this is the sense that we are in relation to another of our kind, that someone is communicating to *us*. Perhaps this will seem less mystical if one thinks of the difference in one's response to a pattern produced by a kaleidoscope and to a child's painting or to a beautiful pebble and to a piece of sculpture. One reason that we do not usually notice this aspect of our experience of literary works is that we are rarely denied it completely, for interesting arrangements of language do not exist in nature and language itself resists the dehumanization that has invaded the other arts. So far, at least, we have scarcely any literary equivalents of the found objects or almost haphazard splashings of paint which are in part the result of aesthetic theories which reject the notion that art has something to do with presence of mind. Those literary experiments, like some of Gertrude Stein's, which involve an extreme and willful curtailment of mind have a labored quality which suggests a kind of perverse mental activity, the mind so to speak, biting its own tail.

When we begin to read a piece of fiction I suspect our most significant initial response is to the mind of the nar-

rator.[3] Whether we go on reading or not and how attentively or respectfully we do so will depend chiefly on
whether we feel the weight of a mind and on how worthy
of attention we find it. Apart from anything else, we will
be sharply aware, first of all, whether our initial encounter
is chiefly with an action or a mind. Consider, for example,
the difference between these two opening paragraphs:

It was 2 p.m. on the afternoon of May 7th, 1915. The
Lusitania had been struck by two torpedoes in succession
and was sinking rapidly, while the boats were being launched
with all possible speed. The women and children were being
lined up awaiting their turn. Some still clung desperately to
husbands and fathers; others clutched their children closely
to their breasts. One girl stood alone, slightly apart from the
rest. She was quite young, not more than eighteen. She
did not seem afraid, and her grave, steadfast eyes looked
straight ahead.[4]

The gulls swept over Dover. They sailed out like flakes of
the fog, and tacked back towards the hidden town, while
the siren mourned with them: other ships replied, a whole

[3] Although I believe that many of the observations I am going
to make apply to poetry as well as fiction, I shall confine my
discussion here almost entirely to the latter. There are several
reasons for this, the most compelling of which is that I have
thought more about fiction. But I believe too, it is more generally
recognized that poems are usually the utterances of particular consciousnesses and are responded to as such. Moreover, the relation
between formal and human elements in poetry and between their
effects seems so varied, complex, and mysterious as to preclude
generalizations, at least until the concept of presence is better
understood.

[4] Agatha Christie, *The Secret Adversary* (London: Pan Books,
1955).

wake lifted up their voices—for whose death? The ship moved at half speed through the bitter autumn evening. It reminded D. of a hearse, rolling slowly and discreetly towards the "garden of peace," the driver careful not to shake the coffin, as if the body minded a jolt or two. Hysterical women shrieked among the shrouds.[5]

There are many obvious differences between these passages and one could easily point to the ways in which the second reveals a more skillful and rich use of language; one might also feel that the second is overwritten; one might, though there is much to suggest otherwise, feel that a mind will eventually reveal itself in the first passage; and we will want to consider later the extent to which straightforward or objective reporting can provide the sense of a mind. But surely what engages one's attention in the first instance is essentially an action, and in the second chiefly a mind. One can almost say we are having two different kinds of experience.

These are extreme illustrations, of course. Not many works begin with as few traces of the narrator as Agatha Christie's; few narrators assert their presence as blatantly as Graham Greene. Nor do we by any means require so extreme an assertion to feel a mind and become interested in it. Almost any sort of trace will do—a touch of boldness, wit, or originality, a mannerism, idea, or bias, or a finely wrought sentence. In fact, any indication that something is being seen from a particular distance or that an

[5] Graham Greene, *The Confidential Agent* (London: William Heinemann Ltd., 1956).

attitude is being taken toward it will convey some sense of a narrator's presence. Many good writers, however, do make a presence felt more immediately and vigorously than has usually been recognized in critical discussion.

The most obvious and dramatic examples, of course, are first-person narratives like *Moby-Dick, The Sun Also Rises,* and *The Sound and the Fury,* in which the narrators are not only presences but characters who are quickly made to reveal themselves as much by their voices and modes of narration as by any other means. But a large number of nameless third-person narrators make themselves felt almost as quickly and effectively. Witness the familiar opening sentence of Jane Austen's *Emma:*

> Emma Woodhouse, handsome, clever, and rich, with a comfortable home and happy disposition, seemed to unite some of the best blessings of existence; and had lived nearly twenty-one years in the world with very little to distress or vex her.

The focus is sharply on Emma, but surely the authority and boldness of the introduction and the striking control of its language make felt another presence as real, in its way, as Emma's. It is not enough to say that we have encountered a style or even a voice. We are aware of a mind at work, of a consciousness not only viewing Emma but feeling and thinking about her. At this point, in fact, we are probably less interested in the girl who "had lived nearly twenty-one years in the world with very little to distress or vex her" than in the narrator who would choose to use quite such words. And though our knowledge of her is not particularized I think we know more about the narrator than we do about Emma.

How different is the narrator who chooses to introduce his hero by telling us:

He was an inch, perhaps two, under six feet, powerfully built, and he advanced straight at you with a slight stoop of the shoulders, head forward, and a fixed from-under stare which made you think of a charging bull. His voice was deep, loud, and his manner displayed a kind of dogged self-assertion which had nothing aggressive in it. It seemed a necessity, and it was directed apparently as much at himself as at anybody else.[6]

Conrad has brought a character into immediate and compelling life, but I am fascinated also by the mind which notices and reports, first of all, how a man advances straight at you, who speaks of a "fixed from-under stare," and who can perceive that a man's "dogged self-assertion" might have "nothing aggressive in it" and could seem a "necessity" and "be directed apparently as much at himself as at anybody else."

Quite another sort of mind makes itself felt as I begin to read *Bleak House*.

London. Michaelmas Term lately over, and the Lord Chancellor sitting in Lincoln's Inn Hall. Implacable November weather. As much mud in the streets, as if the waters had but newly retired from the face of the earth, and it would not be wonderful to meet a Megalosaurus, forty feet long or so, waddling like an elephantine lizard up Holborn Hill.

[6] Joseph Conrad, *Lord Jim* (New York: Doubleday, Page & Company, 1925).

Smoke lowering down from chimney-pots, making a soft black drizzle, with flakes of soot in it as big as full-grown snowflakes—gone into mourning, one might imagine, for the death of the sun. Dogs, undistinguishable in mire. Horses, scarcely better; splashed to their very blinkers. Foot passengers, jostling one another's umbrellas, in a general infection of ill-temper, and losing their foothold at streetcorners, where tens of thousands of other foot passengers have been slipping and sliding since the day broke (if this day ever broke), adding new deposits to the crust upon crust of mud, sticking at those points tenaciously to the pavement, and accumulating at compound interest.[7]

More than by the atmosphere created I am intrigued by the mind that lays it on so thickly, boldly, and delightedly. That I will learn in a few moments that the mud and the murky weather, and especially the fog which permeates every sentence of the paragraph which follows, are peculiarly appropriate to Dickens' theme, makes me even more fully aware that I am encountering not so much a scene as a human vision.

One rather pathetic sort of testimony to the importance of readers' responses to the narrator's consciousness is the advice sometimes given writers to begin their stories in an interesting way and the efforts of fledgling writers to do so. The writer is told to engage his reader's interest immediately and he responds by opening his story with some such observation as "the clock moved remorselessly toward the moment when Jim would have to decide forever between his reason and his passion" or "Seymour

[7] Charles Dickens, *Bleak House* (Boston: Houghton Mifflin Company, 1956).

steadily shadow creeping gains full face in light blast while day dies." He succeeds well enough in making us aware of a narrating mind—a mind striving to be clever or original. And even if the trick works for a few moments we soon discover the qualities of the consciousness that is actually at work.

Almost as self-deluded in their own way are those with interesting minds who think they can hide them or, as Stephen Dedalus puts it, refine them "out of existence." The actual author, it is true, may withhold many of the particular qualities which define him as a person in everyday life, but when we read a book that begins: "Once upon a time and a very good time it was there was a moocow coming down along the road and this moocow that was coming down along the road met a nicens little boy named baby tuckoo. . . . His father told him that story: his father looked at him through a glass: he had a hairy face," [8] or one that begins: "riverrun, past Eve and Adam's, from swerve of shore to bend of bay, brings us by a commodius vicus of recirculation back to Howth Castle and Environs," [9] we feel immediately the presence and force of the mind that has so altered the usual modes of storytelling and language. And we read on with curiosity and excitement because we have experienced not merely an accidentally novel arrangement of words but a mind which will undoubtedly continue to make its presence felt in interesting ways. Or when we read a story that begins:

[8] James Joyce, *A Portrait of the Artist as a Young Man* (New York: The Viking Press, 1964).

[9] James Joyce, *Finnegans Wake* (New York: The Viking Press, 1947).

"Braggioni sits heaped upon the edge of a straightbacked chair much too small for him, and sings to Laura in a furry, mournful voice," [10] or one that begins: "Mrs. Mooney was a butcher's daughter. She was a woman who was quite able to keep things to herself: a determined woman," [11] we feel we are encountering not so much an impersonal or direct transcript of life as a deliberately achieved simplicity and purity, a mind resisting ease and self-indulgence, a mind actively controlling its relation to the story and to us, a mind actively concerned with the material it is shaping and with the act of communicating it. The poise of careful neutrality is a state of mind, not an absence of it.[12]

To encounter a mind as one begins a book, of course, is not always a happy or encouraging experience. After reading a few sentences I know I don't want to be in connection any longer with the mind that proudly labored into being the following:

Indian summer is like a woman. Ripe, hotly passionate, but fickle, she comes and goes as she pleases so that one is never sure whether she will come at all, nor for how long she will

[10] Katherine Anne Porter, "Flowering Judas," *Flowering Judas and Other Stories* (New York: Harcourt Brace & Company, 1935), p. 139.

[11] James Joyce, "The Boarding House," *Dubliners* (New York: The Viking Press, 1968), p. 61.

[12] For another view of the way Joyce moves beyond impersonality and reveals "a recognizable voice," see James McConkey, "The Voice of the Writer," *The University of Kansas City Review*, XXV (December, 1958), pp. 86–87. McConkey goes on to argue, rightly I think, that it is the writer of the slick or formula story who is truly impersonal and invisible and he quotes as an example the opening of a typical Erle Stanley Gardner mystery.

stay. In northern New England, Indian summer puts up a scarlet-tipped hand to hold winter back for a little while. She brings with her the time of the last warm spell, an unchartered season which lives until winter moves in with its backbone of ice and accoutrements of leafless trees and hard frozen ground. Those grown old, who have had the youth bled from them by the jagged edged winds of winter, know sorrowfully that Indian summer is a sham to be met with hard-eyed cynicism. But the young wait anxiously, scanning the chill autumn skies for a sign of her coming.[13]

And were it not out of a sense of duty I would not get beyond these first few sentences:

The sublimity connected with vastness is familiar to every eye. The most abstruse, the most far-reaching, perhaps the most chastened of the poet's thoughts, crowd on the imagination as he gazes into the depths of the illimitable void. The expanse of the ocean is seldom seen by the novice with indifference; and the mind, even in the obscurity of night, finds a parallel to that grandeur which seems inseparable from images the senses cannot encompass. With feelings akin to this admiration and awe—the offspring of sublimity—were the different characters with which the action of this tale must open, gazing on the scene before them. Four persons in all,—two of each sex,—they had managed to ascend a pile of trees, that had been uptorn by a tempest, to catch a view of the objects that surrounded them.[14]

One might object to many qualities of these passages: to the clumsiness of the prose and the sloppiness of the dic-

[13] Grace Metalious, *Peyton Place* (New York: Julian Messner, 1956).

[14] James Fenimore Cooper, *The Pathfinder* (New York: D. Appleton & Co., 1892).

tion, to the pontificatory, complacent, and self-congratu-
latory tone and to the easy, ill-thought-through pronouncements, distinctions, and analogies. But what puts
me off is not so much the individual qualities, per se, as
the minds they imply and convey, minds which instill
anything but liking, interest, confidence, or respect.

As in life, of course, first impressions can be misleading
and there is almost as much variation in the ways narrators
reveal their presences and the speed and directness with
which they do so as there is among people in general. I
have dwelt upon these first impressions partly because
they are often the most vivid and partly to emphasize how
much our initial response to a work may be a response to
a mind.

Before going further I had better make perfectly clear
that the presence or mind I am talking about is by no
means identical with that of the author considered as a
biographical entity. Nor is it an entity separable from the
literary work whose nature one deduces from the work.
It is part of our direct experience of a work and is brought
into being by the work itself. It is a psychological entity
in the sense that we cannot help but feel the presence of
a teller when we are being told something. It is a logical
entity in that the qualities we ascribe to the work such as
style, point of view, structure, pattern, narrative mode, and
especially tone imply a controlling mind. One might say, I
suppose, that the mind in the work originates as the mind
of the author in the act of experiencing and writing his
story, of shaping and being shaped by his materials. Certainly some qualities of his actual mind will be embodied
in the work, and will recur in all his works, but I think it

is more helpful and truer to our experience to think of his presence entirely as an aspect of the individual works themselves. The narrators, say, of "A Christmas Carol" and *Bleak House* or of *The Secret Agent* and *Victory* or of *Sartoris* and *Light in August* have certain qualities in common but our experience is of quite different total entities. Or to put it a little differently, we can say that the presence is given form by the particular utterance and exists in its fullness only within the context of that utterance.

In order to avoid complicating this discussion unnecessarily I have used the terms *author's presence* and *narrator's presence* almost interchangeably and have spoken as though the narrator were always to be identified with the author. A fuller treatment or full discussion of any particular work would need, of course, to be alert to the various divergences and interactions which can exist between the two, to their relative degrees of embodiment, and to the problems raised by the concepts of "mask" and "persona" which suggest there is always some degree of separation. Insofar as the presence I am concerned with is the presence apparent in the particular work, I am pointing to the same manifestation the terms "mask" and "persona" intend to signify. But I do not think the terms sufficiently suggest the dimensions or immediacy of the presence or the extent to which we experience it as a human consciousness.

I should try to make clear also that when I say "presence" or "mind" or "entity" and speak of their "fullness" or "form" I do not mean to say that we experience the narrator as a fully defined human creature. On occasion a narrator may reveal so many qualities that we do in fact construct from them an almost full-blown person and some readers probably almost always construct personages to embody whatever qualities of mind or temperament a work reveals, but the "presence" I am thinking of is generally experienced as something less than a full person or character or apparition—unless, of course, he also happens to be a character in the work.

At the same time, however, the presence, as I hope to show, is usually something more than a mere list of separate qualities and more than is usually meant by the terms "tone" and "voice." And it is something more immediately present, directly felt, and distinctly human than the total set of "norms and choices" in a work for which Wayne Booth uses the term "implied author." [15] Finally, though it should not be necessary after Booth's brilliant discussion of the matter in *The Rhetoric of Fiction*, I should also make clear that narrator presence, as I see it, has very little to do with whether the narrator addresses the reader directly or not. The narrator who scrupulously withholds his own personality, who presumably always shows and never tells, may be as vividly present as what Leon Edel calls "the traditionally ubiquitous and often garrulous nar-

[15] *The Rhetoric of Fiction* (Chicago: The University of Chicago Press, 1961), pp. 70–75. Although I think Booth reduces the usefulness of his term "implied author" by equating it finally with all the moral and artistic choices which have shaped the work and thereby converts into an inference or abstraction what seems to me a presence, his overall discussion of the matter is extremely helpful.

rator who used to interpose his own personality and preachments between the story and the reader." [16] I am more acutely and meaningfully aware of the presence narrating *The Ambassadors* than of the narrator of *Vanity Fair*.

Although there has been little critical recognition of the importance of our response to narrator presence, per se, and of the full dimensions of that response, certain manifestations of the narrator have of course received considerable attention. Endless discussion and lavish complaint have been directed at what has been called the intrusive narrator, and an inordinate amount of time and energy in this century have been given over to celebrating his disappearance. There have also been some able defenses of such narrators and some good discussions of the roles they perform in particular novels. Unfortunately, most of this discussion has tended to equate presence with overt self-acknowledgments and pronouncements by the narrator and to overlook the other ways in which narrators make their presence felt. Even Wayne Booth, who so persuasively demonstrates that presumably invisible authors may intrude and instruct their readers as much as those who comment openly, sees these intrusions as rhetorical establishments of norms and manipulations of sympathies and does not concern himself much with other manifestations of presence or with the reader's responses to them. One wishes also that the various discussions of overt narrators like Fielding

[16] Quoted in Booth, *The Rhetoric of Fiction*, pp. 407–408 from "Introduction," *Henry James: Selected Fiction* (New York: E. P. Dutton & Co., 1953), p. xii.

and Thackeray had concerned themselves with the extent to which the dramatized author—the one who self-consciously addresses the reader and comments upon the progress and meaning of his story—is conterminous with the mind which actually governs and renders the story itself. In poorer novels there are sometimes glaring discrepancies —moralizing narrators whose stories reveal minds fascinated by depravity, narrators who philosophize portentously and tell empty little stories. But even in *Tom Jones,* in which the fusion of talker and teller seems most successful, there are maladjustments and distinctions between the two which would be worth exploring. To some extent the difference is simply that between a mind engaged in a discussion and one imaginatively absorbed in directing and reacting to actions and characters. But differences in the attitudes, values, and emotions of the two also become apparent when one compares, say, the discursive as opposed to the dramatic treatment of either Squire Allworthy or Squire Western. In general, it seems likely that when we say a narrator is intruding on his story, we mean that one sort of presence or mind has intruded upon another.

Considerable attention has also been given—again most notably by Wayne Booth—to the values, attitudes, beliefs, and "norms" of authors and to some of the ways these are revealed, but these have usually been viewed as qualities distinct from a more fully perceived narrator presence and have not been seen as elements which actually convey a sense of that presence. A recognition that we respond to attitudes, values, and beliefs in a work, not as isolated phenomena but as aspects of a more total presence would go far toward answering the recurrent question of how we can and should respond to works based on values or beliefs we do not accept.[17] Much of the reason a non-Catholic can respond almost fully to *The Divine Comedy* and an atheist to *Paradise Lost* is that they are responding to narrators who are only in part defined by their particular values and beliefs. One can enjoy and respect the minds of friends even while they are saying things one cannot accept. One can even love and respect a wife while she is talking nonsense.

Good readers and critics have for a long time been aware of the importance in most literary works of a realm of qualities to which the term "tone" has more or less seemed to apply. The term as normally used has been immensely useful and immensely troublesome, useful because it does draw attention to an author's or narrator's relation to his material and his audience and to his attitudes toward them, troublesome because it does not sufficiently acknowledge that narrator's presence or the full dimensions of that presence and because it has often been seen as the only or the full reflection of the narrator. As has been pointed out many times, the term is a metaphor drawn largely from the realm of speech and purports to describe those qualities of written language which are analogous to those conveyed in speech by inflections of voice. But even in speech, we cannot properly identify any but fairly gross attitudes of the speaker without having in addition to these inflections some fuller recognition of his nature. Inflection alone can convey heavy sarcasm or deep earnestness or extreme playfulness, but

[17] W. J. Ong's distinction, referred to earlier (p. 68) between "belief that" and "belief in" is based largely on such a recognition.

most of the subtler degrees of seriousness or scorn or formality or irony are decipherable only when we are acquainted with many facets of the speaker's mind and temperament. Consider how often others mistake our own inflections or how hard it is to know sometimes just how much even a close acquaintance is joking. Or, at times, to know how much one is joking, oneself. In a literary work, where the inflections, so to speak, are by nature even less easily pinpointed and independent, we require even more acquaintance with the speaker and do perceive and understand the qualities we call tonal as aspects of his more total presence. That is, we respond to them both as components of a larger constellation and as human qualities rather than as merely verbal or stylistic ones. One might say that George Eliot's *Middlemarch*, Cooper's *Pathfinder*, and Ayn Rand's *The Fountainhead* are all narrated in highly earnest tones, but my response is to the earnestness of the particular mind. Consider the following passage in *Emma:*

When it came to such a pitch as this, she was not able to refrain from a start, or a heavy sigh, or even from walking about the room for a few seconds—and the only source whence anything like consolation or composure could be drawn, was in the resolution of her own better conduct, and the hope that, however inferior in spirit and gaiety might be the following and every future winter of her life to the past, it would yet find her more rational, more acquainted with herself, and leave her less to regret when it were gone.[18]

My response here is governed not only by the tone of sobriety, dignity, and restrained sympathy of the particu-

[18] *The Novels of Jane Austen*, Vol. IV, 3rd ed. (Oxford: The Clarendon Press, 1933), p. 423.

lar passage; it is much affected by my awareness of how far the narrator has been moved beyond her usual states of mind and feeling and talking, moved enough to abandon most of the wit, urbanity, and distance with which she normally poses before her characters and readers. The same passage in *Middlemarch*, say, would not be so moving, for it would more nearly reflect the narrator's usual state of mind and feeling. A quiet, speculative passage in a D. H. Lawrence novel affects one differently from a similar passage in one by Thomas Mann.

Much discussion, of course, has also been given to the narrator's "point of view," but again as with "tone," the phenomenon has usually been viewed as a more or less independent aspect of technique rather than as one aspect of a narrator's presence and something which makes that presence felt. In most of this discussion, moreover, point of view seems to have been used in the sense of "vantage" or "observation" point or "angle of vision" rather than to mean "total position toward" or "total attitude toward." That there is a relation between the two is usually acknowledged, but the ways the two affect each other both in general and in specific cases needs far more investigation.

I don't wish to minimize the importance of point of view. For certainly even in its more limited sense as "vantage point" it has much to do with determining the total nature, shape, and impact of a work. Nevertheless, it is but one aspect of the narrator's presence and is always an aspect of a particular presence. It does not, in itself, go very far toward defining the full relation of the narrator to his story or to his readers. This is easily apparent when we recollect, for example, that works with such different narrators as *Tom Jones*, *Middlemarch*, and *Ulysses* are all written by self-conscious narrators using an omniscient point of view. But it is also true of a work with a single point of view in which the narrator has presumably disappeared behind the shoulder or forehead of one of his characters. In saying this I am thinking not only of our sense that the narrator has organized the work or of his precise degree of intimacy or identification with his character or of the times when the narrator cheats a little—as all are sometimes forced to—and slips in his own perception of his reflector; I am thinking also of his direct renderings of his reflector's reactions and even of descriptions of events and characters through his reflector's eyes. Consider, for example, these two passages:

The girl stooped as she came out of the cave mouth carrying the big iron cooking platter and Robert Jordan saw her face turned at an angle and at the same time saw the strange thing about her. She smiled and said, *"Hola*, Comrade," and Robert Jordan said, *"Salud*," and was careful not to stare and not to look away. She set down the flat iron platter in front of him and he noticed her handsome brown hands. Now she looked him full in the face and smiled. Her teeth were white in her brown face and her skin and her eyes were the same golden tawny brown. She had high cheekbones, merry eyes and a straight mouth with full lips. Her hair was the golden brown of a grainfield that has been burned dark in the sun but it was cut short all over her head so that it was but little longer than the fur on a beaver pelt. She smiled in Robert Jordan's face and put her brown hand up and ran it over her head, flattening the hair which rose again as her hand passed. She has a beautiful face, Robert Jordan thought. She'd be beautiful if they hadn't cropped her hair.

· · · · ·

She sat down opposite him and looked at him. He looked

back at her and she smiled and folded her hands together over her knees. Her legs slanted long and clean from the open cuffs of the trousers as she sat with her hands across her knees and he could see the shape of her small, up-tilted breasts under the grey shirt. Every time Robert Jordan looked at her he could feel a thickness in his throat.[19]

A girl stood before him in midstream, alone and still, gazing out to sea. She seemed like one whom magic had changed into the likeness of a strange and beautiful seabird. Her long slender bare legs were delicate as a crane's and pure save where an emerald trail of seaweed had fashioned itself as a sign upon the flesh. Her thighs, fuller and softhued as ivory, were bared almost to the hips where the white fringes of her drawers were like featherings of soft white down. Her slate-blue skirts were kilted boldly about her waist and dovetailed behind her. Her bosom was as a bird's soft and slight, slight and soft as the breast of some darkplumaged dove. But her long fair hair was girlish: and girlish, and touched with the wonder mortal beauty, her face.

She was alone and still, gazing out to sea; and when she felt his presence and the worship of his eyes her eyes turned to him in quiet sufferance of his gaze, without shame or wantonness. Long, long, she suffered his gaze and then quietly withdrew her eyes from his and bent them towards the stream, gently stirring the water with her foot hither and thither. The first faint noise of gently moving water broke the silence, low and faint and whispering, faint as the bells of sleep; hither and thither hither and thither: and a faint flame trembled on her cheek.

[19] Ernest Hemingway, *For Whom the Bell Tolls* (New York: Charles Scribner's Sons, 1940), p. 22.

—Heavenly God! cried Stephen's soul, in an outburst of profane joy.[20]

Although I have tried to select characters and situations which have a good bit in common, there are, of course, important differences between Jordan and Stephen Dedalus and between their situations which do no doubt account for some of the differences between the passages. But the major differences surely arise from the narrators, even though both are presumably confining themselves to a single character's point of view and both are clearly enamored of the girls that are dazzling their heroes. Behind Jordan and Dedalus stand two quite different consciousnesses. They will, of course, have already made themselves felt in more direct and obvious fashion; my point is that even here, where they might be expected to be less visible, they not only shine through, so to speak, but provide much of the quality and flavor of our experience.

Without seeking to define the differences fully or precisely, an effort which is not of moment here, we can say that the second narrator is more lyrical than the first, relies more heavily on repetition and metaphor and uses more elevated and conventionally poetic diction ("bosom" vs. "breast," "sufferance," "gaze"). There are differences, also, in the rhythms of their sentences and paragraphs and in the way they move between their characters. The first narrator keeps his hero sharply in view and moves judiciously back and forth between him and the girl. The second almost forgets his hero in his absorption with the girl. The first narrator is much more aware of color than

[20] James Joyce, *A Portrait of the Artist as a Young Man*, p. 171.

the second, while the second is more concerned with qualities of sound and stillness. The first keeps his characters moving, at what seems a normal speed; the second seeks to freeze the motion and the moment and makes important the shift from stasis to motion. The first narrator registers his hero's emotion as a thickness in the throat; the second as a cry of the soul. And, of course, many more subtle differences might be described.

As we read, of course, we do not isolate individual characteristics as I have done. If the writer is a good one we simply see the characters and events in the form that his consciousness has rendered them. But we are, at the same time, very much aware that we are sharing a particular vision, that the material has been shaped and flavored, that a particular mind is offering us something of its own.

Above I intentionally chose single-point-of-view passages which reveal relatively similar narrator presences. It might be worth looking for a moment at some passages which suggest how much such presences can diverge even within the confines of a single point of view, a single sex, and single century.

His eyes followed her across the room. He saw that the three waiters were observing her, too. She moved like a mannequin, with fluid grace, tall thin, hips slim, thighs and legs long, all elegant and aloof and slithering. As she walked, her legs, close together, provocative, stretched straight before her, the pointed pumps turned slightly outward, her smooth buttocks undulating in the manner of all practiced mannequins. At last, she pirouetted around a corner and was out of view. Straight out of *Elle* or *L'Officiel*, Claude Marceau thought, all haute couture, clothes, face, figure, all glacial and unruffled and not merely mortal. Perhaps it was this that had attracted him first, the challenge of what was or seemed emotionless and unattainable and too near perfection.[21]

The tiles were a faded cherry color, and the toothbrush rack, the fixtures, were ornate, old nickel. The water stormed from the faucet, and Herzog watched as Madeleine transformed herself into an older woman. . . . She did not look at him while making her preparations. Over her brassière and slip she put on a high-necked sweater, and to protect the shoulders of the sweater she wore a plastic cape. It kept the makeup from crumbling on the wool. Now she began to apply her cosmetics—the bottles and powders filled the shelves above the toilet. Whatever she did, it was with unhesitating speed and efficiency, headlong, but with the confidence of an expert. Engravers, pastry cooks, acrobats on the trapeze worked in this manner. He thought she was too reckless at it —going too fast, about to have a spill, but that never happened. First she spread a layer of cream on her cheeks, rubbing it into her straight nose, her childish chin and soft throat. It was grey, pearly bluish stuff. That was the base. She fanned it with a towel. Over this she laid the makeup. She worked with cotton swabs, under the hairline, about the eyes, up the cheeks and on the throat. Despite the soft rings of feminine flesh, there was already something discernibly dictatorial about the extended throat. She would not let Herzog caress her face downward—it was bad for the muscles. Seated, watching, on the edge of the luxurious tub, he put on his pants, tucked in his shirt. She took no notice of him; she was trying in some way to be rid of him as her daytime life began. She put on a pale powder with her puff, still at the same

[21] Irving Wallace, *The Prize* (New York: Simon & Schuster 1962), pp. 15–16.

tilting speed, as if desperate. Then she turned swiftly to examine the work—right profile, left profile—bracing at the mirror, holding her hands as if to support her bust but not actually touching it. . . . She put on a heavy tweed skirt, which hid her legs. High heels tilted her ankles slightly. And now the hat. It was grey, with a low crown, wide-brimmed. When she drew it over her sleek head she became a woman of forty—some white, hysterical, genuflecting hypochondriac of the church aisles. The wide brim over her anxious forehead, her childish intensity, her fear, her religious will—the pity of the whole thing! While he, the worn, unshaven, sinful Jew, endangering her redemption—his heart ached. But she barely gave him a glance.[22]

She came out wearing a reddish-orange wash dress which looked nice on her, because she was dark, curly-haired, with red-fair skin, and the dress set her off just right. And she had on a little powder and lipstick, but it didn't make her look like a sinful woman or anything of that sort. Studs didn't usually pay attention to how girls looked, except to notice the shape of their legs, because if they had good legs they were supposed to be good for you-know, and if they didn't they weren't; and to notice their boobs, if they were big enough to bounce. He looked at Lucy. She was cute, all right. He told himself that she was cute. He told himself that he liked her. He repeated to himself that he liked her, and she was cute. His heart beat faster, and he scarcely knew what he was doing.[23]

[22] Saul Bellow, *Herzog* (New York: The Viking Press, 1964), pp. 110–112.

[23] James T. Farrell, *Studs Lonigan* (New York: The Vanguard Press, 1935), p. 107.

He met her through the MG, like everyone else met her. It nearly ran him over. He was wandering out the back door of the kitchen one noon carrying a garbage can overflowing with lettuce leaves Da Conho considered substandard when somewhere off to his right he heard the MG's sinister growl. . . . Next thing he knew he was clipped in the rear end by the car's right fender. Fortunately, it was only moving at 5 mph—not fast enough to break anything, only to send Profane, garbage can and lettuce leaves flying ass over tea-kettle in a great green shower.

. . . . .

[Riding in the car with her,] he was too afraid for his life to be, as he normally was, girl-shy. He reached over, opened her pocketbook, found a cigarette, lit it. She didn't notice. She drove singleminded and unaware there was anyone next to her. . . . He dragged on her cigarette and wondered if he had a compulsion to suicide. It seemed sometimes that he put himself deliberately in the way of hostile objects, as if he were looking to get schlimazzeled out of existence. Why was he here anyway? Because Rachel had a nice ass? He glanced sidewise at it on the leather upholstery, bouncing, synched with the car; watched the not-so-simple nor quite harmonic motion of her left breast inside the black sweater she had on. She pulled in finally at an abandoned rock quarry. Irregular chunks of stone were scattered around. He didn't know what kind, but it was all inanimate. They made it up a dirt road to a flat place forty feet above the floor of the quarry.

. . . . .

Profane kept running into her in what was left of the summer at least once a day. They talked in the car always, he trying to find the key to her own ignition behind the hooded eyes, she sitting back of the right-hand steering wheel and talking, talking, nothing but MG-words, inanimate-words he couldn't really talk back at.

Soon enough what he was afraid would happen happened— he finagled himself into love for Rachel and was only surprised that it had taken so long.[24]

General Dreedle's nurse always followed General Dreedle everywhere he went, even into the briefing room just before the mission to Avignon, where she stood with her asinine smile at the side of the platform and bloomed like a fertile oasis at General Dreedle's shoulder in her pink and green uniform. Yossarian looked at her and fell in love, desperately. His spirits sank, leaving him empty inside and numb. He sat gazing in clammy want at her full red lips and dimpled cheeks as he listened to Major Danby describe in a monotonous male drone the heavy concentration of flak awaiting them at Avignon, and he moaned in deep despair suddenly at the thought that he might never see again this lovely woman to whom he had never spoken a word and whom he now loved so pathetically. He throbbed and ached with sorrow, fear and desire as he stared at her; she was so beautiful. He worshipped the ground she stood on. He licked his parched, thirsting lips with a sticky tongue and moaned in misery again. . . . He was sick with lust and mesmerized with regret. General Dreedle's nurse was only a little chubby, and his senses were stuffed to congestion with the yellow radiance of her hair and the unfelt pressure of her soft short fingers, with the rounded untasted wealth of her nubile breasts in her Army-pink shirt that was opened wide at the throat and with the rolling, ripened tri-

[24] Thomas Pynchon, *V* (Philadelphia and New York: Lippincott Company, 1963), pp. 23–27.

angular confluences of her belly and thighs in her tight, slick forest-green officer's pants. He drank her in insatiably from head to painted toenail. He never wanted to lose her. "Oooooooooooooh," he moaned again, and this time, the whole room rippled at his quavering, drawn-out cry.[25]

Perhaps the fullest recognition of narrator presence has been provided by the relatively new and undeveloped concept of "voice." [26] The term is a good one in that it recognizes that an author's presence is carried by something more than "tone" and suggests, as McConkey puts it, that behind the work "there exists a human being, a writer with a unique personality and hence with attitudes and values and emotional responses as well as with a typewriter and a textbook by Brooks and Warren and a dictionary which, containing many unusual words, allows him to avoid clichés." McConkey goes on to define voice as something which "emanates not only from the conscious mind but from more obscure sources" and which "is a complex of attitudes, philosophies, and defenses against the world; it has been affected by one's parents and his fifth grade teacher, by the workings of his digestive and glandular juices and perhaps even by a view he once had of the constellation of Orion. Hence voice represents our individual personalities, our response to the world." [27]

But even so broad a concept as "voice" does not suffi-

[25] Joseph Heller, *Catch-22* (New York: Simon and Shuster, 1961), pp. 216–217.

[26] For two especially illuminating essays on the subject see McConkey, "The Voice of the Writer," and Ong, "Voice as Summons for Belief," in *Literature and Belief*, ed. M. H. Abrams (New York: Columbia University Press, 1958).

[27] "The Voice of the Writer," p. 84.

ciently convey the full dimensions of the narrator's presence. If nothing else, by suggesting an auditory frame of reference, it does not point enough toward the qualities we often try to embrace under the term "vision." Nor does it quite aptly suggest those aspects of consciousness that we want to speak of through metaphors of light and illumination. Moreover, as is true of the other qualities of narrators I have been discussing, voice is but one aspect of a narrator's presence and our response to it may be very much conditioned by other dimensions of that presence. I am irritated, for example, by what I can isolate or define as the "voices" of many of Henry James's narrators; and yet as parts of fuller presences whose play of consciousness fascinates me, those voices take on a different sound and meaning.

The term and concept "presence" has its difficulties too, of course, but it does suggest something of the range and multitude of qualities which a narrator may reveal and a reader may respond to, and it does imply that these qualities are human as well as formal and that we respond to them as such. In a moment I hope to indicate something of this range and multitude, but this last point needs some explanation first.

I believe that readers, especially good readers, should, and do in fact, attach qualities they see in the text to a human consciousness and interpret and evaluate them accordingly. We may speak, for example, of a compassionate tone, but what we care about is the human compassion. We will be very much aware if the narrator belies that tonal compassion in other ways; say by manipulating his characters into needlessly painful situations or by dwelling too lovingly on their pain. This is why the sensitive reader finds tear-jerkers so offensive. A smug tone is not offensive qua smug tone. We are offended by it because we dislike smug people and experience that tone as part of a smug human presence. If I am offended by a novel by Ayn Rand, I can describe the qualities in the text which put me off, but what I detest is not the qualities themselves but the mind they make manifest—its pride, smugness, opportunism, and downright bad manners. If I deeply admire most of Conrad's novels, it is in part because I like and respect the way his consciousness works on his materials and because I respond to the very process of his working on them. More. A major limitation of our usual ways of talking about form or even about narrator's functions and techniques is that they make the work a frozen or static entity. Even when we try to show how the various formal elements fit together to achieve the meaning or purpose of the work we do not get the work into motion any more than the naming of the successive positions of Zeno's arrow gets it to the mark. The force which does, in fact, provide the motion, which not only unifies and proportions the various formal qualities but makes them work, makes of them a process and not a collection, is a human consciousness: a mind in action, making its presence felt, making itself known to another human consciousness. If this line of argument leads toward that tangle of misunderstanding and naïveté gathered under the notion of "sincerity," it is probably a mark in its favor, for the persistence of the idea, however much nonsense has been uttered in its name, does indicate how much we do care about the human form embodied in the work.

The range and variety of qualities narrators may reveal are almost as great as those revealed by man in general. The qualities may be moral, intellectual, temperamental, and even sexual. We may be aware of and respond to, among other things, degrees of such particular qualities as energy, elasticity of mind, vitality, self-restraint, straightforwardness or deviousness, orderliness, earnestness, playfulness, self-consciousness, firmness, sensitivity, flippancy, sourness, geniality, glibness, elegance, fastidiousness, scrupulosity, openmindedness, pedantry, toughness, kindness, self-pity, prudery, flamboyance, exhibitionism, shyness, smugness, self-effacement, slovenliness, and many more. We may be aware of a narrator's range of awarenesses and of his major preoccupations or obsessions. We may have a sense also of the way the narrator's mind works, whether it builds slowly and patiently or coils about its materials or juggles them or eagerly rushes at them. We will be sharply aware of a narrator's relation to his characters—not merely his distance from them, but his degree of interest in them, concern for them, fascination by them, or, on occasion, hero-worship, disdain, or even revulsion toward them. We will be sharply aware also of a narrator's relation to us, whether he respects, patronizes, or toys with us. We will almost always notice when an author is violently showing off, whether by learned allusions or set pieces or false modesty or any of the egotistical mannerisms that writers are just as likely to give way to as any of the rest of us. We will be aware also of tiny touches of pretension and self-consciousness, little archnesses and coynesses.

Above all, perhaps, we will be aware of any conflicts, strains, tensions, or ambivalences in the narrator's attitudes, values, or feelings, and as I will argue in a moment, such strains are characteristic of many of the books that interest us most.

No one narrator, of course, reveals anything like all the qualities I have just mentioned. He may be felt as anything from the dim presence of a guiding consciousness of the sort we encounter in an O'Hara novel to the almost fully dimensioned kind of being we meet in *Tom Jones* or, to an only slightly smaller degree, in any novel by Thomas Wolfe. How fully or vividly he is present, of course, will depend on a number of things: on the intensity and interest of the narrative itself—the extent to which our attention is captured by the suspense and drama of the actions themselves; on the sensibility and habits of the reader—the ways he normally responds to presences both in and out of books and the ways he has been taught to read (if taught to look for symbols he will find them, so with narrators' presences); and finally, of course, on the degree to which and ways in which the narrator does expose himself.

Some presences are felt largely because of some one dominant characteristic and almost become reduced to that quality. I am thinking here, for example, of that quality of Graham Greene's narrators which might be described as self-indulgent compassion or of Mary McCarthy's asperity or Hawthorne's gentle evasiveness. Some readers find George Eliot's earnestness so overwhelming that nothing else of her comes through; others react similarly to the smugness of Thackeray or James Gould Cozzens or to the clumsy sincerity of Dreiser or to the tormented exhibitionism of James Baldwin or William Burroughs or to the gentility of Edith Wharton or to the sentimentality of

Dickens. I am not saying that any of these presences need or should be seen as quite so limited, only that they may be perceived as such and thereby profoundly shape our responses to what they are saying. It is also true, however, that we will be most immediately and consciously aware of those narrators who most dramatically and persistently expose one facet of their beings.

Other narrators will be present in fuller, more complex, and less easily definable ways, and even those who seem reducible to single qualities are usually something more than that. If we are to comprehend works in their fullness, we must begin to find better ways of defining and talking about these presences and their effects, ways which will include but move beyond the relatively static and limited, albeit helpful, concepts of author's attitudes, beliefs, ideas or "norms," tone, and point of view, and which will describe more fully and properly the qualities and impacts of particular consciousnesses at work. Above all, and most difficult, we must try to talk more about the texture and, awful word, dynamics of such consciousnesses: the kinds of things they perceive, the ways they perceive and organize, the habits and rhythms and energy of their activities. Hopefully we might sometime be able to talk precisely enough about such matters to distinguish between the presence or mind which informs all of an author's works and that presence which informs any particular one, even to illuminate the distinctions and interplay or tension between the presences of such partly authorial first-person narrators as Jake Barnes, Ishmael, and Marlow, for example, and the presences which put them into motion and continue to hover behind them.

I have no desire to erect any one kind of narrator presence or activity into an ideal; at the same time it does seem clear that many of our most interesting and powerful literary works are those in which the narrator is involved in some form of struggle, in which the narrator becomes not merely a presence but, so to speak, a dramatic entity whose conflicts or tensions as narrator, as teller, become a part of the form and tension of the work. We are interested in part because the struggle adds a dimension to the work and in part because the very existence of the struggle contributes to our sense that a consciousness is, in fact, at work.

Part of the drama of *Paradise Lost* is surely the sense we have of the struggle between the part of Milton that is doing his best to "justify the ways of God to man" and the part of him that belongs to the devil's party without knowing it, and between the side of him that cherishes harmony, order, and obedience and the side of him that admires strain, effort, and achievement. The issue of the fortunate fall in the poem is not, as most critics seem to believe, simply a matter that rests on ideas and doctrine. We feel throughout that the narrator is struggling with the problem and it is the echoes of that struggle and its indecisiveness that help to give the last few lines of the poem their particular impact and meaning.

Our fascination with many Donne poems surely is more than a response to the ideological, emotional, and linguistic strains and paradoxes Donne is manipulating and controlling. We respond also to the drama of a mind moving and working in such a fashion—to its restlessness, to the precariousness of its moments of resolution.

Middlemarch is for many reasons the greatest of George Eliot's novels, but part of its fascination for me lies in my consciousness of the narrator's obviously costly struggle against giving in too completely to her biases in favor of Dorothea and Ladislaw and to her hostility toward Casaubon and Rosamund. That these attempts to be fair are sometimes labored or inadequate makes them all the more poignant, all the more a part of the drama of the work, and they are a particularly relevant part of a drama which is, after all, so much concerned with characters who have difficulty seeing others honestly and generously. It may be somewhat of a distortion to say that the narrator is the central character of the work, but I am quite sure that my deepest response to the work is to that so visibly imperfect and human narrator presence who works so hard throughout the work to be thorough, patient, scrupulous, honest, and sympathetic. That it is hard work and worthy of respect we know in part from the points where she fails so completely, as in her purely sentimental and self-indulgent portrait of Mary Garth and her moments of female cattiness toward Rosamund.[28]

Much of my interest in "Heart of Darkness" and *Lord Jim* comes from my sense of the narrator's and author's struggles to order their experiences, the sheer sense of the struggle itself. In saying this I am thinking only in part of Marlow's and Conrad's self-conscious gropings and speculations, of the sense in which Marlow's confused search

[28] For an excellent discussion of various ways in which George Eliot reveals her presence in *Middlemarch,* see Edwin Kenney, "George Eliot's Presence in *Middlemarch,*" unpublished Ph.D. dissertation, Cornell University, 1968.

for meaning is a part of the structure of the works and a literary device, a way of getting the story rendered. Beyond this, or rather underlying it or within it, one senses a further and not wholly successful struggle—in part a struggle to define the meaning of the central experience of the work and in part a struggle with deeply conflicting feelings and convictions about both the ultimate nature of reality and "the way to be." Viewed in this way some of the contradictory emphases and vague or ambiguous rhetorical fumblings seem not so much flaws as evidences of the severity of the struggle. In contrast, though I am amazed by the perfection and control of *The Secret Agent*, I am less deeply interested, for I encounter there a more comfortable presence who has for the moment resolved his conflicts into a single blend of scorn and pity, and gives no sign of uneasiness about his own presumption of immunity.

One of the qualities of *Sons and Lovers* which makes it at once less coherent and more interesting than many of Lawrence's more "controlled" later works is the narrator's inconsistent or vacillating attitude toward both Paul and Miriam. Seen from one point of view this is a mark of ineptness, immaturity, and lack of control. From another, it is an interesting and moving struggle on the narrator's part to order his feelings and perspectives and the very struggle gives life and interest to the narrator himself. Some other important works with visible narrator's struggles are Crane's "The Bridge," Pound's *Cantos*, Dostoevsky's *The Brothers Karamazov*, Hawthorne's *The Marble Faun*, James's *The Golden Bowl*, Virginia Woolf's *Mrs. Dalloway*, and Fitzgerald's *Tender Is the Night*.

There is a point, of course, reached by works like Melville's *Pierre* and Burroughs' *Naked Lunch*, at which an author's struggle or anguish may become so great that it cannot find a form in which to contain itself or keeps destroying what it creates. Yet the very visibility of the struggle and the destructive record of its intensity may give such works a power and interest beyond that possessed by many more successful artistic achievements.

Insofar as most of the examples above involve a revelation of narrator's struggles through flaws, inconsistencies, and conflicts in a work, the view I have just been taking would seem to challenge our usual valuations of literary order and coherence. In a moment I propose to carry this challenge further. But first it is worth noticing that the entire concept of authorial presence outlined here is one more argument against regarding literary texts as autonomous. That is, if I am correct about the extent to which the experience of a literary work includes an awareness of the teller and a response to him as a human presence it becomes even more artificial to define the work independently of the reader. For if I am correct, literary works require that we respond not only to the words and formal structures themselves but to qualities of mind and temperament that they suggest and reflect. We can, it is true, point to sections of the text which reveal one or another of these qualities, but the presence which gives them their significance can take on its full shape and dimensions only in another consciousness and will be responded to in accord with the particular nature of that consciousness.

If I am correct that in many works narrators and authors' struggles as narrators become part of the form and tension of the work and that we respond to these struggles almost as we would to those of characters in the work, it becomes even less satisfactory to define the reader's role only as a sharing of the author's vision or point of view, for we are also observing his effort to achieve that vision or point of view. Fortunately, as I have argued earlier, readers are complicated enough to hold several positions simultaneously. Just as we can simultaneously identify with and dispassionately observe a character, we can participate in an author's vision and at the same time both share in and observe his struggle to achieve it. And we can simultaneously be critical of his artistic failures and respond to them as measures of his effort and traces of his presence.

Chapter 5

The Discomforts
of Reading

Behind much of the study and criticism of literature is a rarely questioned notion that works of literature, like works of art in general, provide satisfying order and coherence in an otherwise disorderly, fragmented, and confusing universe. Our ordinary experiences, it is contended, are largely formless and incomplete, lacking in meaning. Literary experience, and aesthetic experience in general, are presumably gratifying and pleasurable in great part because they are meaningful, comprehensible, patterned, and unified, or more true, general, or ideal than life. Whether the work of literature is regarded essentially as an overflow of powerful feeling or an imitation of life or an autonomous entity; whether it is thought to reflect objects of sense perception or Platonic forms, particulars or universals; whether its chief function is seen as one of instruction or as one of delight, it has almost always been regarded as providing order, beauty, truth, or illumination lacking in ordinary experience and as providing pleasure or comfort or delight or inspiration largely because of one or more of these qualities. Even those Romantics like Emerson or Shelley who emphasize the constriction and rigidities rather than the lack of order in ordinary experience and the freedom or spontaneity of poetry rather than its coherence, usually regard the ordinary constrictions as uncomfortable and without meaningful form and the poet as offering joy, light, meaning, and even unacknowledged legislation. Even those like John Dewey or I. A. Richards, who attack the notion that aesthetic experience is special and try to relate aesthetic experience to experience of other sorts, continue to emphasize the ordering, unifying, and satisfying aspects of our encounters with literature.[1] And even critics like Simon Lesser and Norman Holland, who concern themselves with the deeper psychological effects of literature and are more aware than some of the discordances, conflicts, and ambivalences in literature, insist that the final effect is to bring reconciliation or equilibrium. Lesser tells us, for example, that art is "an attempt to augment the meager satisfactions offered by experience through the creation of a more harmonious world to which one can repair, however briefly, for refuge, solace, and pleasure." [2] And speaking directly about fiction: "Because

[1] Richards, for example, says that the experiences of the artist, "those at least which give value to his work, represent conciliations of impulses which in most minds are still confused, inter-trammelled and conflicting. His work is the ordering of what in most minds is disordered" (*Principles of Literary Criticism*, [London: Routledge & Kegan Paul Ltd., 1929], p. 61).

[2] *Fiction and the Unconscious* (New York: Vintage Books, 1962), p. 21.

its reference is entirely *internal,* because it winds back upon itself, form deters us from returning from the coherent, comprehensible world it opens to us to the more confusing and frightening real world." [3] Indeed, apart from Plato (for whom art is a bringer of discord, discomfort, and disorder to both the psyche and the state), I can think of very few writers or critics who would not assent to some variety of the formulation I have just been presenting.[4]

This very loose and general formulation, of course, blurs numerous distinctions and oppositions between the various specific expressions of it, whose importance I have no wish to deny. Nor do I wish to deny entirely the validity of that sort of general formulation. In many respects

---

[3] *Ibid.,* p. 185.

[4] A considerable number of twentieth-century artists and writers, of course, believe that art *should* be used to shock, disrupt, irritate, and discomfit and have sought to accomplish this in their own work; but most of these, I believe, would accept the formulation as valid for all traditional art and literature. I am aware of only one extended attack on the equation of art and order: Morse Peckham's *Man's Rage for Chaos* (Philadelphia and New York: Chilton Books, 1965). In this provocative but unfortunately jargon-ridden book, Mr. Peckham argues that art is characterized, above all, by one or another kind of stylistic discontinuity or what he calls "nonfunctional stylistic dynamism." His explanation of this phenomenon is that "the distinguishing attribute of the artist's role is to create occasions for disorientation, and of the perceiver's role to experience it." And he goes on to say that "the distinguishing mark of the perceiver's transaction with the work of art is discontinuity of experience, not continuity; disorder, not order; emotional disturbance, not emotional catharsis" (p. 314). He concludes that art thereby trains our capacity to cope with disorientation in other realms: "Art is the exposure to the tensions and problems of a false world so that man may endure exposing himself to the tensions and problems of the real world" (p. 314).

art and literature should and usually do provide order, form, meaning, and comfort that ordinary experience lacks. Even those like Jackson Pollock or William Burroughs, who use art chiefly to reflect internal and external chaos, can be seen as offering a kind of order, selectivity, and limited truth which ordinary experience does not. Merely to arrest experience, to objectify it in pigment or language, to confine it within the edges of a canvas or the covers of a book is to give it a degree of form and meaning. And it is also true that art and literature provide a way of coping with painful and disorderly things as well as a way of experiencing them.

Nevertheless, there are many aspects of the literary experience and many kinds of literary experience which are not at all in accord with such a formulation and may, in fact, run quite counter to it. That is, the experience of both individual works and literature in general may be an essentially uncomfortable and disruptive one, a movement not toward order and coherence but away from them.

No one who has taught courses in literature needs to be told how often this is true for individual readers. For large numbers of students, the literary work, far from providing welcome and satisfying order, is chiefly a threat and challenge to their customary ways of seeing, thinking, and feeling. It is their ordinary experience which seems to have form and pattern, which seems comprehensible, satisfying, and true. It is their literary experience which is disorderly and confusing, an experience not so much of illumination as of groping in unfamiliar lights and shadows. What they perceive or sense is not the form or coherence of the artist's vision but its foreignness to their own preconceived values and notions and its challenge to the adequacy of their habitual ways of ordering their experience. This kind of response is by no means limited to works like *Walden, Gulliver's Travels,* and Pound's *Cantos,* where the challenge is explicit and direct, and to works by writers like Hopkins, Carlyle, and Faulkner, whose forms are strikingly unusual. In fact, the distinct foreignness of such works may make them easier to accept just as the unconventional or mysterious qualities of a member of an utterly foreign culture may be less troubling and disruptive than the unconventional and unexpected behavior of a member of one's own group. The response I am speaking of may occur toward almost any work which offers or even suggests other ways of knowing, feeling, and being than those to which the reader is accustomed. His own equilibriums may be discomfited by the urbanity of Marvell's "Ode to His Coy Mistress," or by the complexities of Donne's religious attitudes, or by the equanimity of Jane Austen, or by Melville's anguished questioning, or by Pope's orderly anger, or by Whitman's elation, or by Hemingway's code. The very method of ordering experience by means of rhythm, meter, and rhyme remains for some readers, even intelligent and experienced readers, an uncomfortable and disturbing one, as disturbing as the free flow of consciousness is to others. And even quite sophisticated readers may be discomfited by orderings more primitive and simple than their own. Witness the "embarrassment" some modern critics feel on reading Shelley and Whitman. Or witness the hostility between various modern schools of poetry.

My point here, let me emphasize, is twofold. I am suggesting first that the experience of a literary work may involve a sense of disruption and disorder rather than a perception of organization and form. It might be argued that it is the perception of new forms which causes the disturbance and offers the threat, and this may be true to a degree, but the sense of danger, disruption, or conflict is often the dominant one. Second, this experience is often far from pleasant and satisfying. Or at least it is a far more complex mixture of pleasure and pain than it is usually described as being. And this is true not only for those who are especially rigid or who especially fear and resist threats to their particular intellectual or emotional *status quos*. I find hard to understand the endless reiteration of the words "pleasure" and "delight" in literary discussion and am puzzled by the widespread view, here expressed by Reuben Brower, which regards

reading as active amusement, a game demanding the highest alertness and the finest degree of sensibility, "judgment ever awake and steady self-possession with enthusiasm and feeling profound or vehement." Reading at this level—to borrow Coleridgean terms a second time—"brings the whole soul of man into activity." . . . I say "amusement," not "pleasure," to stress the play of the mind, the play of the whole being, that reading of this sort calls for. I am hardly suggesting that literary experience is not a "good," that it is not in some indirect and profound way morally valuable. But if it is to do us any good, it must be fun.[5]

[5] "Reading in Slow Motion," *In Defense of Reading: A Reader's Approach to Literary Criticism*, ed. Reuben Brower and Richard Poirier (New York: Dutton & Co., 1962), p. 4. I should add that although I object to the view expressed in this passage and to Mr. Brower's general appropriation of the word "reading" for what I would regard only as a kind of fairly traditional close

Even if we do not believe Thoreau or T. S. Eliot or any of the countless others who have told us that it is difficult and painful to be more than half awake, surely we know that it is not always very amusing or gamelike or very much fun to have one's "whole soul" or "whole being" brought into activity. It is possible, I suppose, to learn to view the stirring of one's deepest feelings and awarenesses as a game and to regard even *King Lear* or *The Divine Comedy* as the equipment for playing, and it is very easy for teachers and critics to behave as though literary works were merely stones on which to sharpen their own and their students' wits. (It is also possible to forget sometimes that much of our reading can and should be fun. The alternative to the gamester need not be the solemn ass.) But to regard the experiencing of literary works chiefly as amusement or unmixed pleasure or comfort is to be seriously out of touch with much that causes writers to write, with much that compels us to read and study literature, and with much that actually happens when we do.

Even if Aristotle is right about catharsis in tragedy, and we are, in fact, left with a kind of equanimity, the experience of terror and pity is not entirely amusing and the equanimity is of a being which is shaken and drained. Moreover, many tragedies provide little if any catharsis. And even if it is true, which I question, that most literary works do finally provide a vision or form which adequately comprehends or modifies or transmutes whatever ugly, terrifying, or painful elements they possess, surely

---

analysis or explication, he has much that is valuable to say about the importance of allowing students to perform their own explorations of literary texts and about ways of assisting them to do so.

our experience of a large number of works can hardly be described adequately as pleasurable. That a person returns to health after a serious and painful illness does not make the pain inconsequential or illusory. Much of the most compelling fiction and drama, after all, takes us into worlds more frightening, painful, and precarious than our own, worlds in which men find it very difficult to cope successfully with either their fellows or their natural environment and in which suffering is one of the most common occupations. Not only are we unable to close our eyes to the suffering as we normally do in our everyday lives, but we are often compelled to witness it at length and in detail, and sometimes to share it. In everyday life the Gregor Samsas of this world remain nicely disguised in human form and dress; we do not have to watch them drag about their crippled insect selves. In everyday life we are usually spared the tormented soliloquys of Ahab and Lear and even the thinner squeals of pain of a Miss Lonelyhearts or an Emma Bovary. For all of us, surely, there are some works—whether by Euripedes, Shakespeare, Melville, Zola, Kafka, or Faulkner—to which we respond primarily with anguish, and large numbers of works which compel a kind of concern that is anxious and worried. Beneath the anguish or concern, it is true, there may be the comforting awareness that the work is a fiction and that the ugliness and pain form part of a larger whole which modifies or justifies or even transforms them, but this awareness, I think, works something as a faith in God or a divine order does for an actual sufferer's immediate pain. In many works, it is the suffering itself which is etched most deeply in our minds.

It is worth pointing out, also, that even if the psychoanalytic critics are right that literature provides a way of handling or reconciling our anxieties, fears, and emotional conflicts in a protected environment [6] and that literary form is what enables this to occur, it is also true that literature generates and stimulates anxieties, fears, and emotional conflicts and that form serves to sharpen and dramatize them. Again, whatever the final effect, the moment-to-moment experience may be deeply discomfiting. If nothing else, most works generate suspense, which is a form of anxiety, sometimes so pressing that readers will flee to the end of the work for relief.

With poetry the painful elements are usually more immediately, visibly, and continually transmuted into satisfying forms. Moreover, much poetry deliberately excludes the ugly and discordant or has as its direct aim the creation of beauty or provision of delight. And perhaps the differences between poetry and fiction or drama are great enough to make impossible any general theory of literary response. Nevertheless, one's experience of many poems is surely too complex a mixture of feelings to be described as amusement or even pleasure. This is especially true, of course, for poems like "The Wasteland," "The Second Coming," and "Shine, Perishing Republic," which present a particularly grim or disturbing vision, for poems like Hopkins' "Thou Art Indeed Just Lord" or many poems of the contemporary poet Anne Sexton, which are essentially cries of anguish or despair, and for poems like many

[6] Cf. Lesser: "We read because we are beset by anxieties, guilt feelings and ungratified needs. The reading of fiction permits us, in indirect fashion, to satisfy those needs, relieve our anxieties and assuage our guilt" (*Fiction and the Unconscious*, p. 39).

by Hart Crane or Ezra Pound, where the fragmentation
is peculiarly violent and disturbed. But surely the vision or
lyric cry of numerous other poets, especially those of our
time, is discomforting enough to call forth as much pain
as pleasure, to be something other than satisfying. Lionel
Trilling may have overstated when he called Frost's vision
"terrifying," but I do not find it entirely amusing to read
"Provide, Provide":

> The witch that came (the withered hag)
> To wash the steps with pail and rag
> Was once the beauty Abishag,
>
> The picture pride of Hollywood.
> Too many fall from great and good
> For you to doubt the likelihood.
>
> Die early and avoid the fate.
> Or if predestined to die late,
> Make up your mind to die in state.
>
> Make the whole stock exchange your own!
> If need be occupy a throne,
> Where nobody can call *you* crone.
>
> Some have relied on what they knew,
> Others on simply being true.
> What worked for them might work for you.
>
> No memory of having starred
> Atones for later disregard
> Or keeps the end from being hard.

Better to go down dignified
With boughten friendship at your side
Than none at all. Provide, provide! [7]

So far I have been talking mostly of literary experiences involving a high degree of disruption or discomfort. But the traditional formulation is inadequate and misleading in other respects. We need to think much more about the extent to which and ways in which almost any literary experience, even the most pleasurable, involves a disturbance of orders, to which reading is less a rage for order than an escape from it.[8]

One very loose measure of this is the language that is ordinarily used to describe the effects on ourselves and others both of literature in general and of particular works. If called upon to explain why anyone should read or study literature we generally say something to the effect that it stretches, widens, heightens, deepens, broadens, extends, increases, expands, or enriches one's consciousness or understanding or awareness or experience. We speak of new perspectives and deepened insights and widened horizons, all terms which suggest strains of old forms rather than comprehension of new ones. Even if we are embarrassed

[7] From *The Poetry of Robert Frost* edited by Edward Connery Lathem. Copyright 1923, © 1969 by Holt, Rinehart and Winston, Inc. Copyright 1936, 1951 by Robert Frost. Copyright © 1964 by Lesley Frost Ballantine. Reprinted by permission of Holt, Rinehart and Winston, Inc., and Jonathan Cape Limited.

[8] In *Man's Rage for Chaos*, Morse Peckham has made an important move in this direction, and it would be a pity if his heavy reliance on the jargon and conceptions of modern social science denied him a hearing among literary scholars and critics.

by the pretentiousness of such terms and insist on the disciplined aspects of reading we still assent to something of the sort. Individual works are often described as interesting, exciting, stimulating, stirring, moving, or powerful.

Such language is not very precise or illuminating, but it does reflect an important truth about the nature of most literary experiences—that they provide not so much a sense of order or form as of stimulation; not so much a falling into place as a setting into motion; such language suggests that one is not the detached and contemplative observer, but is engaged and activated by the work. However inept or inadequate such metaphors as "stretching" or "deepening" may be, they imply that we do not read primarily either to escape or clarify our confusions or to contemplate order because most of our experience is formless, but rather that our normal experience and consciousness are limited, circumscribed, and quiescent and that we read largely because we want and need those limits challenged, want our equilibrium disturbed.

Our equilibrium or equanimity is no doubt most deeply disturbed by works of great power or complexity, but I think such disturbance is a part of our experience of any work which we actually read and do not greet simply as an old friend, any work in which the sense of familiarity is not the dominant impression. That is, even works whose form is particularly apparent and satisfying, works whose formal structures themselves possess a high degree of order and equilibrium, a sonnet or sestina or set of heroic couplets, are experienced in part as disruptions or agitations and are enjoyed partly for that reason. One's pleasure comes not merely from the contemplation of the form but also from the activity of experiencing the form and from the tension between that activity and one's customary state of consciousness or unconsciousness. In this sense we are shaken up by a sonnet of Sidney's as well as by a howl of Ginsberg's. And depending on one's customary state, one may, in fact, be more disrupted by Sidney. As I suggested earlier, if the disruption is too great either because of the nature of the work or the rigidity of the reader, the experience may even cease to be pleasurable.

The importance of this sense of disruption or agitation is indicated by the desire of both individuals and societies for new works and new forms, a desire by no means limited to those who crave only perpetual novelty and titillation. This desire for change is not so much a desire for new forms, new orders, new meanings, per se, as for the sense of stretching and stimulation the new works provide. This is not to belittle the value of continuing to reread the old. The best of the old never loses its power to stretch and stimulate. And there are important pleasures connected with going back to things which we have fully come to terms with and are fully comfortable with. Still, it is not for this end that writers struggle or readers mainly go to books. The works we value most highly and which most interest us are usually those which are most perplexing, disturbing, or mysterious, those whose complexities, richness, or tensions we are least able to convert into comfortable orders and which therefore can continue to stretch, stimulate, and challenge.[9]

[9] It is also true, as Susan Sontag points out, that we are often troubled by these tensions and complexities—"real art has the capacity to make us nervous"—and that much modern interpreta-

Apart from the element of disruption or strain in any literary experience, and apart from our desire for such strains, is the fact that literature itself is far less ordered, far more disruptive and disturbing than much of our theory and practice assume. This is true of both literature as a whole and of individual works. We have seen as much form as we have because that is what we have been looking for.

There is very little of worth in English or American literature, or in any literature for that matter, which does not in some way work against a comfortable acceptance of the dominant forms of actual thought and behavior in society. When I say this I am not thinking only of directly revolutionary statements or visions such as those, say, of Bunyan, Swift, Blake, Shelley, Emerson, Lawrence, or Henry Miller, to name only a few; nor of works which more or less explicitly attack, mock, or challenge one or more of our institutions, activities, or goals, such as *Walden, Hard Times,* "The Wasteland," or *Death of a Salesman;* nor of works like *Germinal* or *Invisible Man,* which make us witness to some painful spectacle of social injustice. Nor am I even thinking primarily of the fact that there is virtually no literature of value that supports our national dream of salvation through progress (a dream as much shared by universities as corporations), that, in fact, almost all literature directly or indirectly questions that dream. Even Pope and Ben Franklin have things to say which might dismay and complicate life for a progressive young

tion is an effort to escape them, to make art "manageable, conformable" (*Against Interpretation* [New York: Delta Books, 1966], p. 8).

businessman. I am thinking more of the extent to which
literature suggests that most of our major pursuits are misguided or inadequate and that most of our major certain-
ties are suspect or unsound, of the extent to which it
suggests that we are far more "involved in mankind," far
more responsible than we normally acknowledge, of the
extent to which it tells us that we are normally blind to
most of the beauties, terrors, needs, obligations, relationships, and perspectives which lie about us. In sum, literature provides a vision of a world so various, rich, and
complex as to make seem absurd the limited patterns which
particular societies have sought to freeze into reality and
truth and to make seem pathetically inadequate the particular paths along which most of us drift and hurry.

Much that we read, moreover, does not depict a very
reassuring cosmos and more often suggests that "we are to
the gods as flies to wanton boys" than that "God's in his
heaven, all's right with the world." Much literature, of
course, attempts precisely to reconcile us to the presence
of evil, pain, disorder, and death, but many of the attempts bring infernos to more vivid life than the reasons
for them. Elegies are rarely more than half convincing.

I have no doubt overstated my case. I have said nothing
of a large number of works which are almost entirely de-
lightful and reassuring and have ignored much in even the
most disturbing literature which does provide order and
equanimity. But the disruptive and even revolutionary
aspects of literature have so long been ignored that strong
correctives seem in order. For to reduce literature to offerings of comfort, order, and design is to emasculate and
censor it far more effectively than any police state. It

would be better to ban *Gulliver's Travels* entirely than to read it merely as an ironic portrait of Gulliver. Better not to read Whitman at all than to celebrate him for the perfection of a few of his more restrained short poems.

A large number of individual works, even when viewed as formal structures, are also much less ordered, much less unified and coherent, than we usually acknowledge. And an even larger number achieve forms of order which are not so much equilibriums or stable organizations as explosive tensions or precarious suspensions. Robert M. Adams has brilliantly pointed out some of the ways in which and reasons why writers deliberately avoid formal resolution in their works and even strive to provide some major disharmony or impasse, and he demonstrates that a substantial body of literature exhibits some variety of what he calls "open form"—a "literary form (a structure of meanings, intents, and emphases, i.e., verbal gestures) which includes a major unresolved conflict with the intent of displaying its unresolvedness." [10] As major and distinct examples of such a form he cites, among many others, such works as *The Bacchae, Ghosts,* "Ode to a Nightingale," *Don Quixote,* numerous poems of Donne and T. S. Eliot, *A Tale of a Tub,* Kafka's "Metamorphosis," "Song of Myself," *The Counterfeiters, The Sound and the Fury,* Jack Kerouac's *On the Road,* and *Finnegans Wake.* Among writers who have produced works with some significant open elements, he mentions Shakespeare, Molière, Chekhov, Pirandello, Brecht, Tennessee Williams, Stendhal,

[10] *Strains of Discord* (Ithaca: Cornell University Press, 1958), p. 13.

Flaubert, Tolstoi, James, D. H. Lawrence, Virginia Woolf, and Gertrude Stein.

Adams is careful to remind us that "few or no literary forms are completely closed on every conceivable level" (p. 15) and he cautions critics against too eager a pursuit of open elements. "With a quick eye, a keen nose, and a mediocre amount of determination, the critic who wants to can easily discover an element of openness in almost any literary form. If it is not an ideological or emotional issue left unresolved, it may well be a narrative thread left untied, a sequence of images unlinked to other sequences, or a narrative framework casually overstepped by authorial comment. That these elements are insignificant provides no sure recourse from critical inquisitions. Once alerted to the concept of ambivalence (which is, on a small scale, very much what openness is on a large one), what incredible trophies have not the devoted critics produced!" (p. 201).

Although I think a fairly intensive and widespread critical hunt for open elements may be needed to counteract the long-time quest of the closed, Adams is certainly right to remind us that the concept of openness can be misused as any other. Nevertheless I think open form plays an even larger role in literature than Adams suggests and that there are significantly open elements in a majority of the works which most interest us. And I am speaking now not of the strains and tensions that result from the stretching of consciousness or from a clash between the values or attitudes of a reader and those of the work, but only of strains and irresolutions inherent in the works themselves.

Fully to support this contention is beyond the scope of

a book concerned mainly with relations between the work and the reader, but let me suggest briefly what I mean by pointing to some examples of significant open elements in works not necessarily of enough overall openness to have warranted Adams' attention and some examples of significant unintentional openness which he excludes by definition.

A number of works, more or less closed in some respects, are informed throughout by tonal ambiguities or equivocations or by a speculative and ruminative quality which has somewhat the same effect. This characteristic is exhibited most consistently and strikingly, though quietly, by Hawthorne, for whom the words "maybe," "perhaps," and "might" take on an almost talismanic quality. It is marked also in Melville, Conrad, and Faulkner, especially in their narrators and sometime spokesmen Ishmael, Marlow, and Gavin Stevens, each of whom loves to guess, to offer alternative hypotheses and paradoxes, and to cast doubt on his own observations. Each of these authors in at least one work—Melville in *Pierre*, Conrad in "Heart of Darkness," and Faulkner in *Absalom, Absalom!*—moves beyond mere ambiguity into uncertainties and undercuttings so violent and crucial that scarcely any ground remains from which to comprehend them.[11] The most extreme instance of narrative self-destruction I have encountered is Beckett's *Molloy*, whose first-person narrator can scarcely utter a sentence without casting immediate doubt on its validity. Henry James is less frank about his lack of frankness than the writers so far named and his method is to hint rather

[11] For an excellent discussion of this matter, see James Guetti, *The Limits of Metaphor* (Ithaca: Cornell University Press, 1967).

than hypothesize or theorize, but most of his works exhibit a generally ambiguous and evasive quality as well as some central ambiguity with respect to a character's motives or perceptions. As Adams points out, in one work, at least, *The Sacred Fount*, he, too, moves beyond ambiguity to an openness so fundamental as to crumble the ground under its own and its reader's feet. Some other writers whose tone is frequently ambiguous, or at least elusive, are Swift, Chekhov, Emily Dickinson, E. M. Forster, Joyce, Nabokov, Robert Frost, and Genet.

A considerable number of works are fractured by the writer's inability either to escape or to confront directly some important problem or conflict. The work raises the problem in such a way that the reader cannot ignore it, but fails to grapple with it adequately. Whether or not one is horrified by the latter portions of *Huckleberry Finn*, a matter I have already discussed at length, and whether or not one wants to call it a great novel, one can scarcely fail to ask where Huck or anyone can go when the river or adolescence runs out, and one can scarcely fail to hear the hatred not merely for corrupt society but for the whole "damned human race" that Twain cannot yet directly confess. At the end of *A Connecticut Yankee in King Arthur's Court* neither the reader nor Twain, nor anything in the book, can explain why there should be quite so many corpses.

Thoreau, like Twain, can find no proper form for the hatred and contempt he sometimes feels toward the human species or for his sense that his experiment was both a success and a failure. He asserts that his aim is to wake his neighbors up and his Chanticleer crow is, in fact, sufficient to interrupt one's sleep, but he has almost nothing to say about how an awakened man can live in society. In different ways, Melville, James, and Hemingway, like Twain, educate or exhibit their heroes away from the American shores and seriously propose questions about "how to be," but do not ever let their heroes come home again. Any respectful reading requires us to ask how Ishmael and Strether manage after their returns and how one can live all the way up or even halfway up in Sheboygan, Ithaca, or New York City. The works barely suggest any answers. Edith Wharton will not ponder substitutes for the societies she so skillfully demolishes. Emily Dickinson will not quite take hold of the question which burns throughout many of her best poems—whether eternity is heaven or merely the painless tomb. Emerson will not recognize the difficulties of following both Carlyle and self-trust, and it is not merely a little mind bedeviled by the hobgoblin consistency that must wonder whether he is advocating the assertive nonchalance of little boys sure of their supper or the passive faith of the eastern mystic. My examples so far suggest that this and other sorts of openness are especially common in American writing. Some of the reasons for this are obvious enough but the matter could well receive more attention.

Among major English writers, the chief example of this sort of more or less unintentional openness seems to me to be Dickens. He not only cannot decide but cannot really even debate with himself whether the evils he depicts in *Hard Times, Bleak House,* and elsewhere are rooted in political and social institutions or in human hearts, and whether they require revolution or philanthropy. Neither ending of *Great Expectations* really confronts the question on either a narrative or theoretical level of where to go or how to be when you discover what your expectations were made of.

Another sort of openness—which rarely appears more than momentarily in good writing but is unhappily common elsewhere—is a major incongruity in the work of which the writer is unaware. One variety of such openness might be labeled "Martial Christianity" or "I'll-bash-your-head-in love" and would include that vast array of poems, stories, sermons, and hymns which celebrate the lamb with the voice and spirit of the tiger. A mild example is the hymn "Onward Christian Soldiers." Other varieties are drawing-room primitivisms and pretentious celebrations of simplicity, epitomized in action by Marie Antoinette's pastoral productions and in literature by numerous pastoral poems and by eighteenth-century novels like *Oroonoko;* prurient or sadistic moral tracts; pompous assertions of humility of the sort one finds in Joyce Kilmer's "Trees" and an unkind critic might find in e. e. cummings' attention-claiming disclaimer of self-capitalization; and totalitarian clamors for freedom like those of Ayn Rand and Mickey Spillane. Less distasteful, but similarly incongruous to my mind, at least, is the sort of mechanical production of mystery in poems like Poe's "The Raven" or "Ulalume" and in most so-called Gothic novels.

The most common and important form of partial openness, however, is provided by what might be called the countercurrents within a work—some element in it, of structure, point of view, tone, attitude, pattern, or meaning—which runs against the main drift of the work. Even properly to introduce this matter requires far more space than I can give it here and the subject itself is worthy of book-length study, but let me simply mention a few such currents, some of which I have touched upon already in other contexts: the generation of sympathy for Shylock in *The Merchant of Venice*, the minor motif in Hamlet (not a major one as G. Wilson Knight would have it) that associates Hamlet with sickness and Claudius with health, the partial attractiveness of Satan and the suggestions of a fortunate fall in *Paradise Lost*, the suggestions in *Emma* (outlined but greatly overemphasized by Marvin Mudrick [12]) that Emma has hardly learned a thing, the suggestions of Allworthy's blindness and stupidity in *Tom Jones*, the modest undercutting of Dorothea and the attempt to be fair to Casaubon and Rosamund in *Middlemarch*, Wordsworth's egotism in *The Prelude*, the unreliability of Nelly Dean in *Wuthering Heights*, the suggestion in *Lord Jim* that Jim's final heroism is a repetition of his original failure, the elements of free will and moral choice in the novels of Dreiser and other naturalists, the curious vitality of the language and rhythms in T. S. Eliot's "The Hollow Men," the undercutting of Paul in *Sons and Lovers*, and the challenges to Jake's values in *The Sun Also Rises*. The reader can no doubt supply many more examples.

One might argue, of course, over the strength or importance of any particular countercurrent. My point is simply that a great many works, especially those which interest us most, are less closed and unified than much of our criti-

[12] See *Jane Austen: Irony as Defense and Discovery* (Princeton: Princeton University Press, 1952).

cism indicates. The strength of our desire to see closures is indicated by the fact that every time a critic discovers a countercurrent he tries to insist that it is the main stream.

Apart from these various sorts of strains which are sufficiently severe to warrant a label like "open," there are the strains inherent in many of the organizations and relationships which we think of as providing pattern, order, and unity—inherent, that is, in antithesis, in paradox, in contrast, in modes such as the mock heroic, tragi-comic, or pathetic comic (e.g., Faulkner's "Spotted Horses"), in the varieties of structures that fall under Joseph Frank's definition of spatial form, in irony, and in metaphor itself. This point is too obvious to press very hard and there has perhaps been too much tendency in some quarters to reduce everything in literature to tension, but it is worth reminding those who like to contrast life's disorder with the order of art that very often the elements pulled together in literature are also flying apart, that what we call fusions and reconciliations could very often more adequately be defined as juxtapositions, yokings, and suspensions, and that at least as much of the power of literature comes from the *effort* to fuse, reconcile, and pull together as from the achievement itself. The effort is apparent in great part through the strains that remain visible. One last point. Unity, harmony, resolution, pattern, and order in literature are very often experienced as intensity and excitement. The work or some part of it comes to rest, but we are moved.

Chapter 6

Against
Detachment

I SPOKE earlier of the various degrees of human susceptibility to the roar of pain that lies on the other side
of silence and presented as an extreme of deafness and
wadding of sensibility Vittorio Mussolini's perception that
a group of Ethiopian horsemen resembled a rose bursting
into bloom as a bomb exploded in their midst.[1] The most
extreme, and possibly absurd, alertness to the roar on the
other side of silence is perhaps that of Ivan Ivanych in
Chekhov's story "Gooseberries." Ivan has become so horrified by his brother's foolish and piggish complacency
that he becomes incapable of watching happiness without
an "oppressive feeling bordering on despair."

"I said to myself: how many contented, happy people there
really are! What an overwhelming force they are! Look at
life: the insolence and idleness of the strong, the ignorance
and brutishness of the weak, horrible poverty everywhere,

[1] See above, pp. 82–83.

overcrowding, degeneration, drunkenness, hypocrisy, lying—
Yet in all the houses and on all the streets there is peace and
quiet; of the fifty thousand people who live in our town there
is not one who would cry out, who would vent his indignation aloud. We see the people who go to market, eat by day,
sleep by night, who babble nonsense, marry, grow old, good-
naturedly drag their dead to the cemetery, but we do not
see or hear those who suffer, and what is terrible in life goes
on somewhere behind the scenes. Everything is peaceful and
quiet and only mute statistics protest: so many people gone
out of their minds, so many gallons of vodka drunk, so many
children dead from malnutrition—And such a state of things
is evidently necessary; obviously the happy man is at ease
only because the unhappy ones bear their burdens in silence,
and if there were not this silence, happiness would be impossible. It is a general hypnosis. Behind the door of every
contented, happy man there ought to be someone standing
with a little hammer and continually reminding him with a
knock that there are unhappy people, that however happy he
may be, life will sooner or later show him its claws, and
trouble will come to him—illness, poverty, losses, and then no
one will see or hear him, just as now he neither sees nor hears
others. But there is no man with a hammer. The happy man
lives at his ease, faintly fluttered by small daily cares, like an
aspen in the wind—and all is well." [2]

As always in Chekhov, who is wiser than all his characters and usually seems wiser than all the rest of us, there
is much which casts reflections on the particular character
and particular view, and there is much which makes us
smile at Ivan. Among other things, he more than anyone

[2] *The Portable Chekhov,* ed. A. Yarmolinsky (New York: The
Viking Press, 1947), pp. 380–381.

else in the story seems able to be happy, and much in the story—especially the lovely maid Pelageya—challenges Ivan's view. At the same time Chekhov's irony turns more sharply against Ivan's companions, who understand nothing of his story, and especially Alyohin, who "did not trouble to ask himself if what Ivan Ivanych had just said was intelligent or right" and is pleased because Ivan was "not talking about groats, or hay, or tar, but about something that had no direct bearing on his life." [3]

Vittorio Mussolini is so distant and detached from the violent event he is observing that he cannot hear or feel the actual screams that accompany it. Ivan Ivanych is so alert to inaudible screams of pain that he cannot bear even happy and peaceful scenes. From Vittorio Mussolini's point of view, ugliness has been transformed into beauty, become esthetically satisfying. Ivan Ivanych's vantage point makes ugly and discordant what is apparently happy, peaceful, and quiet. Vittorio Mussolini has seen pattern in a scene which a participant or involved observer would experience as profound disorder. Ivan is so acutely tuned to a disorder or reality behind appearances that he cannot accept the pattern or order which directly confronts his senses. To adopt Mussolini's point of view requires the observer to feel that he is immune, is in no way involved in the scene he is observing. The Ivanych view implies that everyone is so implicated in the world of suffering that they should never for a single moment be allowed the privilege of forgetting that implication.

These specific comparisons are suggestive, I hope, but I offer the two visions not so much as direct analogues to

[3] *Ibid.*, p. 383.

those of writers or readers, as to represent two very general extremities of human response by which much that we think and do can be measured. From one point of view the two extremities are equally insane and a proper or ideal human point of repose or tension would be somewhere between the two. From another point of view, which I have to believe is shared by most of us, the vision of Vittorio Mussolini is a horrifying one we would wish to label callous, inhuman, or insensitive, while the Ivan Ivanych vision, however foolish or self-destructive, has a certain beauty and appeal and might be labeled oversensitive, oversympathetic, quixotic, or even saintly. Viewed thus, the proper or ideal human response would be an effort to move away from the first view toward the second, or to use George Eliot's terms, to try to be as attentive as our wadding of stupidity allows to the roar which lies on the other side of silence. Despite the example of a few martyrs we need not fear that very many of us will ever become thinly wadded enough to die in the effort.

Now I do not want to say that our dominant modes of viewing and teaching literature put us in Vittorio Mussolini's aesthetic camp, but I do think they do more to make the Mussolini vantage point tolerable than they do to lead us toward saintliness or martyrdom. I shall devote some space to explaining why this is so, but my assertion may seem less outrageous for the moment if we remember that professionally (objectively? scientifically?) speaking, the image of the opening rose is not horrifying, callous, and unhuman, but merely reflects a narrative stance involving an unusual degree of distance and detachment. Professionally speaking, one might say that Ivan, on the other hand, shows an abnormal lack of perspective. Our professional tools and knowledge encourage us to talk about the ways in which distance reveals pattern and beauty. They do not, in themselves, encourage us to view distance as a potentially dangerous ideal. My assertion may also appear less strange when we remember how attractive and comfortable distance is. Distance *is* much more likely to make things in both art and life appear orderly and beautiful, to obliterate discordances and blemishes. Distance allows us to be spectators and contemplators of spectacles in which actual or emotional involvement would be painful or dangerous. Distance helps us to achieve that contemplative ideal which has always been a compelling one for those fortunate enough to be able to afford it.

In the event the Mussolini analogy sounds too much like calling fascists all who disagree with me, let me put the matter another way and say that if the Ivan Ivanych position would entail the foolishness of converting literature into no more than a collection of little hammers and wadding penetrators, our dominant course is to view and teach it in such a way as to make it harmless to our heads and thick skins.

I have already touched in other contexts upon many of the ways this palliation is assisted. Insofar as we divorce the study of literature from the experience of reading and view literary works as objects to be analyzed rather than human expressions to be reacted to; insofar as we view them as providing order, pattern, and beauty, as opposed to challenge and disturbance; insofar as we favor form over content, objectivity over subjectivity, detachment over involvement, theoretical over real readers; insofar as we worry more about incorrect responses than insufficient ones; insofar as we emphasize the distinctions between literature and life rather than their interpenetrations, we reduce the power of literature and protect ourselves from it.

The alternative to this direction and these emphases need not be a full-scale retreat to lax impressionism or a conversion of the study of literature into moral instruction or psychotherapy. We need not abandon the quest for knowledge and the attempt to transcend the personal and contingent. These have their own beauty and virtue as well as their inadequacies and dangers. The alternative can be a sharp recognition of these inadequacies and dangers and an attempt to nurture a counterforce in both criticism and teaching.

The recognition I am urging should include not only an awareness of the theoretical and critical difficulties of the sort I have been dwelling upon throughout this book —the discrepancy between the languages and modes of literature itself and the languages and modes we usually use to talk about it, the gap between the experience of reading and the usual emphases of literary study, the impossibility of determining the relative importance of elements of a work so long as we ignore effects on readers, the overemphasis on pattern and unity, the relatively limited extent to which a literary work controls responses, the enormous complexities of actual human perception and response, and the impossibility for the reader to become merely a passive sharer of authorial point of view. It should include also a sharp awareness of the fact that distance, detachment, impersonality, and objectivity have affinities not only with certain kinds of truth and beauty but with indifference, complacency, callousness, and finally inhumanity; an awareness that while it would be intolerable to view the world perpetually through Ivan Ivanych's eyes or to maintain a critical and classroom atmosphere in which Buchenwald and mushroom clouds were always relevant, it is a kind of insanity to create and dwell in atmospheres which make such perspectives and recollections ill-mannered and irrelevant. Above all, I believe, we need to recognize where the clear and present dangers lie.

Despite the present unrest on many college campuses and a variety of challenges to traditional patterns of education, it does not appear to me that many substantial changes have occurred in the way we think and talk about literature. It does not look as though we were in great danger from too much impressionistic or passionate criticism and scholarship, from too many essays in our professional journals like, say, those in D. H. Lawrence's *Studies in Classic American Literature* or like Virginia Woolf's "Mr. Bennett and Mrs. Brown," from too many teachers who so anguish over what writers are saying that they ignore the ways they say it, or from too many students who become dangerously involved in the works they are studying or write papers about how writers have changed their lives or who so confuse literature and life that they rush out of their classrooms to tilt at windmills. There is little danger of stumbling over people so awed or moved or excited by what they have just read that they aren't looking where they are going.

Surely we are in much greater danger of our scholarship and criticism becoming more and more of an industry which produces products with no individual stamp or conviction; from a proliferation of articles and books in which the literary works examined might as well have been any other sort of object or commodity; from too many classes in which books and poems are no more than historical documents or assemblages of formal components or else gymnasiums for what is sometimes called an intellectual workout; from students whose responses are not so much incorrect as thin and mechanical and whose papers seem perfunctory exercises, not much distinguishable from one another; from students who have either stopped responding to what they read as full and complex human creatures or else do so but haven't learned how to manifest it or else have dissociated their actual literary experiences from their schoolwork. Many of them learn very well how to bring methods to bear on literary works—how to talk about structures, how to trace themes and patterns of imagery— and how to compare literary works with one another. Very few have learned how to bring their experience to bear in such a way as to deepen the work and make it matter. Many acquire large vocabularies for analysis and explication; if forced to talk or write about their actual experience and response, few are able to move beyond primitive terms of like and dislike. Many have learned to remain almost entirely untouched by what they read.

By way of counterforce I have no wish to offer a program or set of directives. We have enough of these already. What we need to develop is a varied body of criticism and knowledge which starts, first of all, with the assumption that the critic is a particular human being with glands, sense organs, and emotions as well as an intellect and a body of learning, and, second, with the recognition that what the critic has to tell us about is neither the work itself nor the effect of the work on him but his experience of the work. The sort of critic I am thinking of would be sharply aware of what took place during his act of reading and might well describe changes in his experience in successive readings or differences between his experiences while reading and reflecting upon the work. If he has found, for example, as I have, that over the years the pain in many of Emily Dickinson's poems has come to seem less poignant, more verbal and contrived, he might talk about this and explore the reasons for it, both in the poems and in himself. If he has had the experience, as I have, of discovering as he began to give a prepared lecture on Edith Wharton's *House of Mirth* that the book which had moved him deeply the night before had overnight cheapened itself and died in his consciousness, he might abandon his notes and try to explain what had happened and why. Such a critic would try to be aware of his biases and open about them, and he might well wonder aloud at times about their effect on his literary experience. He might well confess to unreasonable hostilities or indifferences. He might even, at times, confess to being puzzled or ambivalent. Such a critic need not necessarily be as personal and lyrical as a D. H. Lawrence or as cantankerous as an H. L. Mencken or as passionate as an Eldridge Cleaver—though these are fine ways to be. He might sound more like Henry James or Mark Van Doren or the students whose papers I have appended to this book.[4] The main thing is that he would sound like *somebody*, and if not a particular somebody, at least a recognizably human creature.

[4] See Appendix.

While I would hope this sort of critic would have some knowledge and common sense, he would be less concerned with thoroughness and "soundness" than with talking about what really engaged him about a work. While reading Conrad's *Victory*, for example, if he had fully realized for the first time that Heyst virtually rapes Lena at the end of their discussion of the Morrison affair (Chapter 4, Part III), and had become infuriated by Heyst's inability throughout the preceding and following scenes to comprehend her fear and insecurity, he might want to talk about those scenes at length: tracing in detail the steps by which that grateful and submissive girl could come to sign "imperiously to him to leave her alone" and that so-considerate gentleman could ignore both her tears and her command. In so doing the critic might give vent to his own indignation at the same time as he tried to assess the narrator's view of the matter and the relation of those scenes to the tragic events which follow. And he might write such a piece before his indignation had cooled and the scenes had faded into their proper place in the total canvas. Or such a critic might ignore the differences between Faulkner's *Light in August* and Ellison's *Invisible Man* and the full complexities of each work in order to trace with concern the ways each shows how black psyches are damaged: as Ellison puts it, "hurt to the point of abysmal pain, hurt to the point of invisibility." And he need not hesitate to ask himself and his audience to ponder whether the Invisible Man was wise in trying once more to emerge from underground or right in saying, "you won't believe in my invisibility and you'll fail to see how any principle that applies to you could apply to me. You'll fail to see it even though death waits for both of us if you don't." If at some moment in his life the critic fell uncritically in love with a particular poem or book, he would risk the embarrassment of simply singing its praise.

The chief problem for such critics would be to find ways of talking about responses and about the movement and life of literary works which were neither private and jargonish on the one hand nor banal on the other. The chief temptation for such critics, of course, would be self-indulgence: to block the work with his own presence or to convert it into his own navel. Nor does the sort of criticism I am urging provide any insurance against mediocrity and dullness. But neither does anything else. It might reduce pomposity a little and help some critics who now express what are surely their opinions in the tone of eternal truth to find more becoming voices. Finally, I must insist that the kind of criticism I am urging must not be categorized as undisciplined or irresponsible. Some of it will be, but surely in a profession which purports to value imaginative literature it is strange to equate discipline and responsibility only with impersonality and scientific procedures and to distrust criticism as it moves toward art.

I wouldn't want to see this sort of criticism supplant the impersonal; I really wouldn't; but there is no reason why it can't coexist with the other, even within, say, the pages of *PMLA*, which when it does admit the human voice admits it only in the clubby tones of its "For Members Only" section. The most widely circulated journal in our profession need not go on creating the fiction that books are objects and documents only, or remain one of the world's chief repositories of the passive impersonal voice.

With respect to teaching, I hesitate to use a word like counterforce because it suggests movements, doctrines, methods, programs, and curricular changes. And the kind of changes I am looking for can come about only through individual teachers becoming sufficiently unhappy about the present relation of students and texts to try in various ways to make that relation more meaningful. I say "sufficiently unhappy" because it is clear that the majority of teachers are far from satisfied with their accomplishments. They want their students to read with greater depth of feeling and understanding, want them to feel that literature is more relevant than they do, want them to feel that their experience with a body of literature is not just one more three- or four-credit course. But the outcome of this more or less collective discontent is rarely more than an endless tinkering with course offerings, honors programs, and the like. There are many reasons, both human and administrative, most of them obvious enough, why the changes go no further than this. Among these, of course, is the understandable, and in many ways essential, belief in the worth of organized and objective knowledge and the value of impersonal intellectual discipline—a belief which, let me repeat, ought not to be abandoned but only continually challenged and discomfited by values of other sorts. Nor do I see much present danger of it being abandoned. We are hardly at the point where more of our students are writing poems than term papers or where the balance of power has shifted so that universities allow only a few scholars-in-residence.

Among other hindrances to effective change, two, I think, are crucial and need some discussion. The first is the fact that our present failure is not very dramatic; our customary emphases and structures work after a fashion. The second is the belief that the only alternatives are flaccid and self-indulgent "appreciation" and idle chit-chat.

Viewed in the midst of our daily activities about the school or university or amidst a committee not of persons but of colleagues and with neither books nor students in sight, our programs and courses and achievements seem reasonable enough and our failures seem inevitable. It is hard to remember all sorts of things we really know. It is hard to remember how many students we turn out who are really untouched by having taken our courses. It is hard to remember that upon graduation most of them stop reading little more than trivia and go on to live their lives, both inner and outer, as though nothing had happened to them. It is hard to remember that almost everything about a classroom, about the relation of student and teacher, about the structure of the curriculum—in short about the total environment in which we teach literature—helps to produce this unhappy condition and is at best alien and at worst hostile to the fullest comprehension and experiencing of literature. By this I mean mostly that all of this defines a world in which literature is not really relevant except as a subject matter for study and in which a full literary experience is not likely to take place. Perhaps this will seem a less outrageous thing to say if one imagines a student sitting at a desk in a row of desks at 9:44 on a Tuesday morning with the class to end in six minutes, at which time he will have to rush to physical education or psychology class, trying to consider seriously the meaning of the lines "Ripeness is all" or "In every voice, in every ban, / the mind-forg'd manacles I hear." He has to hold himself reasonably aloof; he has to respond with only a small and temporary part of himself or he might well forget to copy the next day's assignment or to get to his next class. He might weep or exclaim. He might quit school altogether for a week. He might, after reading a poem about the desperate loneliness of all people, take hold of his neighbor's hand. The teacher, however informal, however warm and sympathetic, however stimulating or wise, however fully responsive to literature himself, is an employee of an institution who is hired to teach a certain number of hours a week and to give students grades.[5] At the end of the hour he must usually vacate the classroom and as often as not rush off to meet some other obligation. Whatever his natural bents, he is usually under some external and internal pressure to provide coverage rather than depth. He has material to "get through." He must talk to or with a *group* of students; his relation must be to the group rather than the individual. Most of his talk and the talk in the classroom must, perforce, be public talk. The only responses he can be concerned with are public ones or at least verbal ones. He has no way of acknowledging or evaluating a pregnant silence or gleam of understanding, to say nothing of "thoughts that lie too deep for tears" or of "internal difference / where the meanings are." In short, literature in the curriculum and classroom becomes essentially subject matter to be studied and talked about like other subjects and other matter. In such an environment

[5] If this seems to give undue prominence to the function of grading I might point out that almost the only thing most universities absolutely compel faculty members to do is to give grades.

it comes to seem an entirely reasonable act to ask about Auden's line "We must love one another or die" *only* how it relates to the rest of the poem or what its meter is or to reproduce it as an item on an identification quiz.

It is hard, in this institutional environment, to remember how little our organized instructional activities have to do with the central purposes for which literature is written and read. Our main activities within the academy go toward taming and institutionalizing it. Through this process we do throw light upon it and encourage minds to give it serious attention. But it is the kind of light and attention that most often tends to isolate and even seal it off from both the inner and outer worlds in which our students really live.

This brings us to the second hindrance to effective change—the belief that a concern with the reader's experience and with the relation of literature and life can lead only to idle chatter, bull sessions, and loose and undisciplined noises or silences of "appreciation" and preference. And there is, of course, some reason for such fear, for much trivia, nonsense, and intellectual laziness and haziness have been supported under the slogans "experience" and "life." I am going to argue in a moment that such concerns can, in fact, lead to intellectual activity which is just as demanding, disciplined, and challenging as any other, but it is worth pointing out first that while silence, inarticulateness, and confusion on the part of our students may indicate a lack of sufficient response and understanding, they may not mean that at all and may sometimes be signs that the experience has been particularly meaningful, complex, or full. It is well to remember, also, that almost

all teachers—by selection, by training, and by the purposes
of the institutions for which they work—are deeply biased
in favor of the stated, the rational, the articulate, the orderly, the explicit, and the precise, and find it difficult to
keep sharply in mind that these qualities almost always involve a reduction of experience and reality and a certain
sacrifice of richness, complexity, and truth. And the
teacher of literature is no exception even though much of
what he teaches directly or indirectly challenges that bias.
Although he knows, as A. R. Ammons so succinctly puts
it, that with the creation of a work of art "a world comes
into being about which any statement, however revelatory,
is a lessening," [6] his chief direction is away from the work
toward statements about it and he is more likely to strain
for precision than for truth or to assume that the precise
is the true. Perhaps most difficult for any teacher or critic
of literature to combat is his tendency to concentrate upon
the qualities of a work or literary experience for which we
have or can develop clear languages and to overlook those
aspects of the work or experience it is more difficult or less

[6] "A Poem is a Walk," *Epoch*, XVIII (Fall, 1968), 115. Mr.
Ammons goes on to say: "I appreciate clarity, order, meaning,
structure, rationality: they are necessary to whatever provisional
stability we have, and they can be agents of gradual and successful
change. And the rational, critical mind is essential to making
poems: it protects the real poem (which is non-rational) from
blunders, misconceptions, incompetences; it weeds out the second
rate. Definition, rationality, and structure are ways of seeing, but they become prisons when they blank out other ways of
seeing. If we remain open-minded we will soon find for any easy
clarity an equal and opposite, so that the sum of our clarities
should return us where we belong, to confusion and, hopefully,
to more complicated and better assessments" (p. 116).

interesting to talk about. This is true, of course, in all realms of inquiry. People talk about what they know how to talk about and find interesting to talk about. But again our dilemma is peculiarly acute since so much that we study asserts the value of untranslatability and is valuable largely because it resists definition and because many of its most priceless qualities are the most elusive. While it is true that any teacher or critic who relied very long on terms no more precise than "life," "power," "mystery," "moving," "intensity," "richness," "atmosphere," "color," "movement," "complexity," "tone," "interaction," "sincerity," and "uniqueness" would be a bore, it is also true that the moment he moves very far from them his activity will be guided more by forces, rules, interests, expediencies, and vocabularies arising from his professional and academic environment and his need to formulate than by the nature of literary works and experiences themselves.

Still, so long as we are teachers, critics, and students— so long, in fact, as we are humans—we need to talk, and literature is valuable and fun partly because it gives us something to talk about, because it does challenge us to formulate and express our responses and experience and does provide the opportunity for brilliant or deeply thoughtful articulation. I want to insist, therefore, that a concern with the reader's experience and the relevance of literary works need not lead to idle chatter and vague impressionism. On the contrary, it can stimulate intellectual inquiry of the most interesting and demanding sort and, what is more, lead to formulations which are both more meaningful and more accurate than those which are presumably "objective."

One reason so much talk about experience and relevance has been unsatisfactory is that it usually moves in a single direction—away from the work. Instead of remaining an essential and inextricable part of the experience that is under scrutiny, the work becomes mere stimulus or introduction and the attention turns entirely to the state of the reader's psyche or environment. Moreover, these states themselves are often not so much scrutinized or defined as loosely asserted or emoted about. This need not be the case, for there is no good reason why the same pressure cannot be exerted in the definition of such states as in the explication of texts. No good reason why one cannot define one's responses to Jake Barnes as carefully as one can the significance of his wound or talk as well about the effects of the "I"–"you" dialectic in Whitman's poetry as about his use of biblical or oratorical rhythms. Nor is there any reason why the work itself cannot be held sharply in view, especially when it is defined as part of an experience rather than as an object separate from it. Questions about response will then turn back naturally toward the work, and a discussion of reactions to Jake would certainly lead to questions about the extent to which these responses are in accord with the work and about how they are shaped by the book. By starting with actual responses to the scene in which Mike taunts Cohn for being a "bloody steer," one might well begin to see the full complexities of the characters' attitudes and relations to one another and avoid the kind of misreading that imposes on the work such patterns and labels as "in-group," "outsiders," "initiates," and "Hemingway code." Conversation about the precise tone of Jake's final "Isn't it pretty to think so?" might engender a more meaningful investigation of the book's affirmative and despairing qualities than would a discussion of the implications of the title and epigraphs. Similarly, a discussion of responses to Whitman's "I" and "you" could hardly fail to illuminate some of the most important aspects of his work.

The approach I am urging here, like any other, can be converted into a patronizing pedagogical device, one in which concern with response becomes merely the carrot to draw the student into supposedly more objective or sophisticated considerations. But it has the advantage of conforming to our natural lines of interest and curiosity and of accommodating our changing experience of a work. It is, in fact, my ambivalence toward Jake, the odd mixture of admiration, respect, pity, irritation, and contempt I feel for him, that pulls me back to the book so often and makes me want to listen more attentively, makes me want to understand what sort of narration it is and to distinguish between the moments of more and less controlled narration, between the superficial and real callousness, between the self-conscious and unwitting revelations of his suffering, and between his glib perceptions and his deepest ones. I really want to know exactly how he sounds—the precise mixture of flatness, bitterness, anger, self-pity, and resignation—as he says at the end, "Isn't it pretty to think so?" And I can only find out by going back to the text.

I want to know how reliable a narrator Jake is not because I want to understand the technique of the novel, but because I have to know in order to make better judgments and better order my responses and because I really want to know whether Hemingway is sharing various of my feelings and judgments. Whether he shares my view, for example, that Jake is a somewhat lazy fisherman and that the whole fishing episode is somewhat tainted, whether he attaches as much importance as I do to the old waiter's disgust over the goring of the young farmer. If my interest in this last leads me to notice how Hemingway emphasizes the young man's funeral and the existence of his widow and two children and how he reminds us of the goring in the last four sentences of the chapter, I am excited not primarily because I have learned more about the technique and structure of the novel or even about author intention as such, but because I am better able to experience the work and because Hemingway has revealed his presence.

When Whitman addresses me, I do, in fact, experience an uneasiness and sense of resistance which makes me want to examine the question further, both in the text and in myself. I want to look back and examine the various ways he has used the word "you" and the various qualities of my response to them. I want to know when and to what extent I resist because I am hearing rhetoric rather than a person, or because I do not think he really includes one so unrobust and academic as myself, or because I have never liked the sensation of another man's arm around my shoulder, or because I am personalizing the term more than he intended, or because to an inhabitant of twentieth-century America his dream has to have a hollow and dated sound. He says he saw us as later riders on the Brooklyn Ferry and we were to connect with him and one another by having the same experience: "Just as you feel when you look on the river and sky, so I felt" and "I considered long and seriously of you before you were born." But I can't forget that the ferry is gone and that he did not consider long and seriously of us riding through tunnels in our cars. But neither can I escape the question whether this dates him or us and the question whether my own uneasiness about his embrace isn't additional evidence of our need to listen to him.

Another reason for the unsatisfactoriness of talk about experience and relevance is that both the proponents and critics of such an approach seem to talk as though the relevance must be to immediate social and political issues of the day or to the immediate social, psychological, or economic goals, interests, and problems of the reader. It is true there are certain moments when such immediate concerns are so pressing for an individual or group that any discussion which fails to consider them will seem deliberately or coldly evasive. Nor, as I have argued earlier, is undue involvement the most dangerous or unbecoming human condition. But surely life and experience need not be so narrowly defined. Life and experience are also ways of feeling, acting, and talking and the cumulative understanding, knowledge, and awareness that a human being has acquired. It is these to which literature has its chief relevance and with which it must connect. One cannot even read without making some such connections, without bringing some experience to bear, and without the work having some reverberation within that body of experience, but for most students these connections are minimal or thin. The difficulty is not so much that the students' experience is insufficient as that they are not sufficiently aware of its relevance to the work and the work's relevance to it.

When they read Thoreau's *Walden*, for example, they may need help to feel the full impact and relevance of Thoreau's metaphor of sleep and awakening. It is not enough to point out or ask them to point out the brilliant elaboration of metaphor by which he moves from his proposal "to brag as lustily as chanticleer in the morning, standing on his roost, if only to wake my neighbors up" to his final "Only that day dawns to which we are awake. There is more day to dawn. The sun is but a morning star." It might be well to ask the students to think or talk about how it feels to be sleepy as against fully awake and to think about the kinds of occasions on which they were most fully awake and about the people they have known who struck them as most fully awake. And they might wrestle for a while with the question "Why is it that men give so poor an account of their day if they have not been slumbering?" They could be encouraged to think about the kinds of occasions on which they awakened without alarm clocks as they read that "little can be expected of that day, if it can be called a day, to which we are not awakened by our Genius, but by the mechanical nudgings of some servitor." Should it occur to the students that they wake sometimes from anxiety or fear as well as from "force and aspirations from within," they might go on to examine the distinction between sleeplessness and being fully awake and might be urged to talk about the sufficiency, validity, or persuasiveness of Thoreau's view of the human psyche. It might also be well to remind students that Thoreau's metaphor is by no means a dead or literary one and encourage them to think of examples of it in their own idiom ("Come on, wake up"; "Rise and shine"; "You're asleep on your feet"; "Dimwit"; "It dawned on him"; "He saw the light"; etc.). In such a discussion it would be important, of course, for the students to understand that their knowledges and psychological experiences were not necessarily to be equated with Thoreau's full meaning and that he was widening and stretching our usual conceptions of the common terms. And one would wish to encourage the students to go on to explore the extent and nature of that widening and to think about the extent to which Thoreau could be called a mystic and about how and how well he makes his appeal. One would wish them, finally, to consider what the purpose of the book was and what it asked of them.

It is remarkable how many students, and teachers too, read a poem like Frost's "Stopping by Woods" with its lines, "The woods are lovely, dark, and deep, / But I have promises to keep / And miles to go before I sleep / And miles to go before I sleep," [7] without feeling the poem has any relation to them, without even wondering whether or not they have made the same choice. It might help them to think and talk for a while about the kinds of woods, both literal and figurative, external and internal, which they have known that are lovely, dark, and deep and about why they have gone on past. And while I would hate to see the poem perverted into an excuse for talking about the problem of drugs, some talk about such trips into woods might

[7] From *The Poetry of Robert Frost* edited by Edward Connery Lathem. Copyright 1923, © 1969 by Holt, Rinehart and Winston, Inc. Copyright 1936, 1951 by Robert Frost. Copyright © 1964 by Lesley Frost Ballantine. Reprinted by permission of Holt, Rinehart and Winston, Inc., and Jonathan Cape Limited.

help make the poem matter more for many students. Some thought and talk about their own degree of ambivalence about staying on the road and keeping the promises might help them better gauge and want to gauge Frost's tone and degree of acquiescence, and might make them want to read other poems by Frost and others which turn on similar choices. It might also help the teacher to remember and confess that he, too, has stopped by woods, and left them unexplored.

Obviously, there is no easy way to deepen the kind of awareness I am urging, especially since much in the very nature of schools and classes works against it. Such awareness can, however, be fostered even in the classroom through discussion which recognizes at the outset that the locus of the event under examination is neither the reader nor the text alone but the intersection or communion of the two. Such discussion would take its shape from the particular humans involved in it. It would start with or at least dwell upon and explore the actual responses of the particular readers, including those of the teacher, and seek to test, educate, and deepen these responses rather than label them right or wrong. It would accept the validity of tensions and maladjustments between the reader and the work. Finally, it would be deeply attentive to the work itself, and it would be conducted with as much care, intellectual rigor, and sympathy as the group was capable of. Hopefully, such discussion would lead, on the one hand, toward a fuller illumination of the work and finally a truer set of statements about it, since it was no longer a theoretical construct but functioning and in motion, and, on the other, toward individual experiences of the work which were worthy of the term "experience," experiences in which the work became a part of a life and world and not merely an item in a curriculum.

In practice, of course, the two ideals cannot be as comfortably balanced as in the rhetoric of the preceding sentence. As the history of criticism and education clearly demonstrates, either the work or the reader will tend to recede or disappear as there is concentration on the one or the other. What I am preaching, finally, is only that we learn how to hold the two in better and more fruitful tension.

At this moment in time, to gain that tension, it is the reader and his experience which require special concern in theory, in criticism, and in the classroom. We have learned quite well how to get our students to produce intelligent but colorless and impersonal analyses and explications. We do little to encourage or teach them to write essays of the sort I have represented in the Appendix, essays which, however imperfect, reveal human beings in active relation to an author or work. We train our students quite well to talk perceptively about the structure, patterns, and meaning of a work; we do little to help them to talk well and carefully about the conjunction of the work and their experience. We are quite good at recognizing and challenging ignorant and inappropriate responses; we know little about how to encourage and measure fullness of response.

We have developed elaborate vocabularies for classifying and anatomizing literary works; we scarcely know how to talk about their powers and effects. We have an immense accumulation of knowledge about authors, periods, movements, and individual texts; we know almost nothing about the process of reading and the interaction of man and book.

We have an astronomical number of assertions that literature is not life and should not be confused with it; we have almost nothing to say about the danger of separating them, the danger of viewing literature in such a way as to make of it an object which we can manipulate instead of a force which can help to shape us.

We have recognized the values of detachment and the dangers of undue involvement. We have not been very mindful of the relations between detachment and coldness and between involvement and love.

The direction I am proposing has not many paved roads or signposts; it does not offer the enticements and consolations of impersonality, detachment, and easily discernible order; it is even questionable whether it will lead to much that looks like knowledge, as that word has usually been defined. It does allow us, however, to examine, if not the real locus of the literary work, certainly the point at which it kindles into an event, and it does allow us to touch, explore, wonder at, and wander over the full complexity of the terrain. Finally, it allows us to do these things without forcing us to be something other than the quite human creatures we are who turned to the study of books because we liked the experience of reading them.

*Appendix*_____

Two Papers
by Students

Impressions of Emily Dickinson*

by Sylvia Lewis

I CAN see Emily Dickinson because part of her is in me. She doesn't talk to me; she doesn't talk to anyone. Her poems are hers alone, not ours. She writes them to keep the bomb calm, to keep the top of her head in place, for the same reason that she so carefully thinks about tying her hat, creasing her shawl, or baking bread for her father.

She is private, alone, separate. And she doesn't want me, she doesn't want to meet me, she certainly doesn't care to have me read her poems. But she is civilized, polite. She herself admits that no one could understand her agony, the hurricane in her soul, because her face and manner protect her. They are the best watchdogs of her feelings. Her mind is a house, dark, shut, private. Its rooms are hidden from us, and only she can know them, in desperate moments when her loneliness or anguish must confront

* Written for a course in Whitman and Emily Dickinson, Cornell University, May 1967.

themselves, and she must release them into poems. But she can never confront me with her suffering because it is too intense. Nor does she want to expose it. She is thankful that it is subterranean. And she is proud. To be public is to be common, and dirty somehow. Emily Dickinson could permit herself neither, since her isolation is regal and exclusive, not imposed by others. She chooses to be separate, the queen of her own despair, both she and it in white.

If she doesn't want me, how can I want her? I would feel like an intruder if her poems—only some of them—were not also mine. And they are. Not because I have suffered as much as she, or because I am as sensitive and intense a person as she. It must be a matter of degree. Perhaps there is too much of Whitman in me. Like him, I have to be outside, to travel, to see a shift of faces, to expect connection with another person, sexual or otherwise. Nature is never bees and flowers or a "narrow Fellow in the Grass" (E.D., 389). It is mountains and stink weed in a small stretch of wood and running naked through a creek when the stones slash at the soles of your feet. I am not as refined as she, but neither is my unhappiness so dignified, nor so well expressed. Hers is agony, each part of it pinned down and examined before she can find some comfort or calmness by writing about it. Mine is usually self-indulgence.

What difference would it have made to Emily Dickinson if she had read *Leaves of Grass?* She might have been shocked by Whitman's blatant sexuality and repulsed by his philosophy of brotherhood because it makes him and all those he describes common. Perhaps she would frown at his generosity with words, which might seem to her to be irreverence for them. And where is his God? Of course she cannot be sure of her God either, since in His jest with her He often seems to be hiding or passively approving acts of cruelty. Yet her God is almost a person, a banker or father who allots her occasional portions of happiness. She can relate to Him as to any other distant friend—through thought, affection and faith in His continuing love, though the faith gnaws; doubts prod at the edges of her consciousness. She could not know Whitman's God, who is not a separate person, but the soul-body of all men and all life, everything "beautiful, wondrous, or lustrous."

Whitman wrote his poems for her, as he wrote them for me, to tell us we are loved and fine and beautiful, though we may not think so. I know he would love her for her physical delicacy and whimsy and her soul strength, over-looking her pale skin, her lack of health and robustness. But what if he should look past her, simply including her in his catalogue of faces? It would not be her fault entirely, if in fact it were a fault at all. For the two of them could never talk. She would not believe that he sees her, because she is separate and hidden from his poems, as we all are. Perhaps Whitman knows that part of his soul is in her, and in me. Perhaps it is. But Emily Dickinson knows just as surely that her soul is only her own, and I believe her. Thus I can say that part of her is in me, but what I am really saying is that I see myself in her poems. She whispers to me that she creases her shawl to keep from exploding, and I do the same. But why? Neither of us will tell why, and Whitman can never know.

Yet in one corner of his mind, Whitman understands

this. He acknowledges privacy and separateness, because he sees it in himself. To the potential lover, the reader, he warns:

Do you see no further than this façade, this smooth and tolerant manner of me?
Do you suppose yourself advancing on real ground toward a real heroic man?
Have you no thought O dreamer that it may all be maya, illusion?

> (From "Calamus," When I Heard at Close of Day)

Is he not also questioning himself? And are these questions so unlike Emily Dickinson's asserting,

> Far safer, through an Abbey gallop,
> The Stones a'chase—
> Than Unarmed, one's a'self encounter—
> In lonesome Place—
> Ourself behind ourself, concealed—
> Should startle most—

> (E.D., 274)

The difference lies in the intensity of caring. Whitman can dispel his self-doubts by submerging himself in love relations, by finding one face in the crowd that cares, if only for a night. He can still celebrate. But Emily Dickinson has only her self, and she must suffice. Her pain seems constant, though formalised and refined through poetry, the poetry that knits her mind in place. Possibly, then, she neither accepts nor needs Whitman. Does he perhaps need her?

Whitman*

by James Moody

Through the house comes the smell of large spring raindrops,
steaming on the warm earth.
I hear the warm spring rain blown by the wind against loose
windows.
The dark spring rain splashes off my shoulders,
outside bringing in the things that can't get wet.

* * *

I HAVE a feeling that Whitman is a self-made poet, much like the self-made man he celebrates. He is a poet, they are miners, carpenters, professors, farmers, accountants, they are all men, all common poets. Whitman would rather be remembered as a man first, then as a poet. The way any man is absorbed entirely in his job, his job becoming most of his life, what he tells his wife, his dreams, the paint that never washes out of his knuckles, coal soot always in his lungs, so Whitman made poetry his job, bringing it into

* Written for a course in Whitman and Emily Dickinson,
Cornell University, May 1967.

daily life and making all our world apt subjects for poetry
—poetry would no longer be reserved for the cream of life
—the "higher" feelings.

* * *

Driving to New York alone without a radio.

Each house is different and much more than just shelter.
Each colored many-shaped house is a part of who's inside.

I see a white house with freshly painted sides, newly
built, surrounded by two new cars, bright new grass, an
antenna for the TV. After it a three-story house, solid and
old, surrounded by tilting porches and old trees with tire
swings, once white clapboards peeling and fraying to the
natural wood, their yard is brown with old grass, ruts
from junk cars and leapfrog. Next, a piece-meal house
part lean-to, part trailer, the refrigerator outside where
there's more room, a broken tricycle, a rusted wagon, a
yard full of old rusting cars, a heap of soggy garbage,
swings tipped over, a motor cycle, a mother carrying a
baby. On their land too is a barn red barn, empty and falling down at one end.

They are all the same to Whitman. They are all part of
the American Land and its people. Regardless of their
individual fates, troubles, joys, Whitman celebrates them
as pure images of the Land, as fine as a mountain horizon.

Man has bought the land and shaped it his way. Hills are
shaved off, then forests, fields plowed, yards planted,
marked with out-buildings, broken fences, road signs,
corn, junk cars, pipe lines. The Land is equal in splendor
to an untouched Northwest Vista.

Driving along I can't see it this way. I can only experience the facts and the individual hardships and wish more for them all. I wish them into the suburbs, into apartments. I see the beauty, energy, life of Route 79 through Caroline, but can't believe the simple happy life is possible any more, I want electric lawn mowers for them, chaise lounges, barbecues, a new car.

Whitman would hate that. He celebrates their life as much finer. But I still feel he sings too much, he drives past too fast, sees it all as a general image, praises too indiscriminately.

I love his style of putting things down and not worrying how they mean. He feels that's all, and the best thing a good reader can do is feel back. The names of the things, the lists of rivers, people's occupations, joys, do not mean anything specifically, but we all associate feelings and experiences with them. We know what a farmer means, we know what city means, what clerk means. They're in no order, rather blatant disorder, complete disorganization —not juxtaposition. Reading some sections, you might think he's trying for meaning by juxtaposition—by contrast—but I'm sure not. They are extremes of feeling, not meaning, and it's easy to see through the things to the man who is calling them up, from what he saw, and from what he, a poet, wants to be true. To believe Whitman goes without saying, since most of the time he deals in concrete things we can readily imagine, or have seen for ourselves. "Song of the Open Road," verses not written for libraries, not even to be read, simply written for the joy of writing —and for the things that are the true poems. He says this 100 times—men are the poems, women, children, trees, lies, dreams, engines, celery, fear, rain.

To read Whitman is to read about your own day, any yesterday.

Yesterday, I shot a sparrow with a B.B. gun and killed it. I wanted more than anything not to kill that bird who would live 2 or 3 more years, and be happy or sad, however is the way with birds, or be cold and hungry, or warm and full in the Southern sun, to make love or talk to a good friend—whatever is their way. I crept up to within 25 feet. I was talking to a friend, a girl who said I'd never hit it because there were too many branches in the way. I pulled the trigger of the stupid plastic and tin gun and the bird fell from the thin branch, dying in the air, wings tangled. All she said was My, wasn't I a good shot.

Standing over it in the field its death meant more than when my grandmother died. My friend was worried about the chill breeze and asked for a sweater.

To kill a deer for meat is strong friendship among men, a mile apart in the empty winter forest, walking parallel, stalking the game, the snow silencing the sound of the deer's run.

To kill a pheasant in the air, at dawn, and to have a wife who will make it lunch, is to be rich and part of the land. To shoot a duck in the pond, even if it has a wife and memories of long summers is good if it brings men close over an outdoor fire smiling between the delicious swallows of dark meat.

To crush the copperhead about to strike you, to set an iron trap for the weasel who has killed your chickens, is survival and will never bother man's conscience, to poison rats and swat flies is instinct.

But who are the men that put kerosene rags in their

lobster pots to capture every lobster for a mile, who poach deer with flashlights, who catch baby sharks from their yachts, slit their bellys and throw them overboard, who drown cats and shoot sparrows with B.B. guns?

Whitman isn't willing to listen to the reasons, or rather he takes them for granted, and moves on. The bird sings to him in "Sea-Drift." The acute sadness he feels for the vanished bird's mate turns to gay expectancy, as he vows that somehow he will try to make up for all the sorrow and death in the world.

They are all characters in Whitman. The hunter is no better than the poacher, the shark killer no worse than the woman who puts down the rat poison. They all have reasons. None are more evil than others. Death is to be celebrated as just another part of life.

Thinking of the sparrow, I think of the bird in "Out of the Cradle Endlessly Rocking." What was most important was not the death of the bird but the power of the experience to draw me out into a seldom reached world where the commonest things are seen anew with vast meaning and worth. Killing the bird meant much more than killing the bird. And it is this way for Whitman. The dead bird serves only as the trigger to show him all the mystery and pain, injustice and faith in the world. The fate of death causes so much to happen in his mind that it is worth the loss of life.

It seems to be the key to his poetry—he lets everything affect him to the furthest extent. We all do it to some degree: mentioning a city can recall the time I lived there, the home I lived in, a friend next door, the day I threw the hammer at him, the apologies and tears and the smell of the hospital. One forgets it all, forgets everything about the city, the home, the friend, the hammer. But every hospital you are ever in will smell like the one from that time. That's how Whitman's poems work in us as well as in him. Things lead to other things, until, far away from the poem, with no comment from Whitman, finally you know exactly what he means. The joy of being able to light up and say, "Yes, I feel it, I know exactly how he feels, happens all the time." Whitman's experience can become yours.

In a "Song of Joys" he puts so much together in one place. He knows one man very well, himself, and from him he can know the joys of firemen, fishermen, drunks, boys, soldiers.

Once I rode a slow train for days and nights into the Yucatan jungle plotting on my maps where the lost city should be. It was at the fork of two rivers and would be an easy 3 days walk from the train's last stop. I dreamed a year of the vine-covered temples, dreamed of coming on it at night, silhouetted against a full moon, spent all summer looking for it and remembered nothing of the whole year but the day I was to fly home from Merida. The plane that was to take me originated earlier in the day at Lima and would end at London that evening. I would take it as far as New York. It landed and as I walked toward it on the hot runway, a girl came down the first class ramp, fresh from the air-conditioning, her hair thick and wild from a long sleep, yawning, stretching in the sun. She was the most beautiful girl I have ever to this day seen. We passed on the runway. I took my seat anxiously watching if she was to board again. I imagined her rich life, London to Lima and back—the noise of the crowded plane, all languages, mixed into silence as I found her in the crowd. From a distance she was painfully beautiful. She walked back to the plane, boarded it by the separate first class ramp. I sat in that plane for 5 hours knowing she was feet away, unapproachable, impossible. Getting off at New York, I waited for her, hoping we could meet and our lives would change, but she didn't get off and I watched the plane leave for London.

It's a mad new world that strangers can see in each other the image of a dreamed-for lover and meet and love as strangers. The girl in the plane will mean more to me than any wife, any lover. The men and women in the city are the same to Whitman. What is it about love and desire that eclipses all else? To bring away from a city ("Once I Passed through a Populous City") only memories of loves, to bring from a summer only a girl's face.

Whitman celebrates the power and creativeness of man, alone, in "On the Open Road," "Song of Occupations," "Crossing Brooklyn Ferry." Whitman holds as sacred a man's life with himself, in his day's work, and his strength to be able to carry it out. Women ruin this. Women ruin poetry, ruin work. There is nothing to be done but make love. No poems can be written, no paintings finished, no appointments kept. Men throw away everything for love. "When I Heard at the Close of the Day" is a fine example. Nothing, neither fame, nor success, honor, means anything to Whitman if he can't have the love of his comrade.

So Whitman, happily, contradicts himself. Life is a contradiction and never constant—Jarrell says, "what controlling, organizing, selecting poet has created a world

with as much in it as Whitman? A world that so plainly is
The World," and he himself says, "There are no poems,
just people."

* * *

"Song of the Answerer"

An outcast, laborer, senator reads Whitman and takes
faith. Until the poem he is sure that a man must be what
he is, not hide it, defend it, sing it. Black, farmer, homo-
sexual, Republican, stupid, artist, liberal, scholar, de-
formed, whatever, it is man's right. Prejudice is certainly in
Whitman's catalogue of evils.

And then there is the Answerer.

And what if we are like the Answerer? Is it the best
way? I can talk to scholars, carry the right books and pass
the tests. I can strip to my T-shirt, shoulder the jack-
hammer and talk like my fellow laborers. In coat and tie
I crawl under the car with the mechanic to show him the
trouble and talk in his language of springs and gaskets. At
a soirée, I can laugh after cocktails, at the van Gogh in
the closet, or the backless Betsy Johnson dress. The
Answerer is no hypocrite, nor insincere. He is hung up
on taking on the character of those he's with so that he
will fit in. He knows their way of life more than his own
—he's trying to be considerate. He takes off his coat and
tie and rolls up his shirtsleeves before going into the general
store, so as not to seem too good for the store. He combs
his hair for his father, cuts it for the bartender, puts on
dirty clothes for the mechanics, searches for a small bill
for the toll collector. He hides his own light, not because
he is afraid to listen to his own drummer, but simply to

please others. They will never accept him if he is at all different, so he conforms to whatever they are, and in the end, he destroys himself. Not one person thinks him at all original, he is just like them. His real world suffers, his own world disappears. It seems there is no other way to get along.

Stranded on the road, waiting for my car's fuel pump to be repaired, we hid from the bloody cold in a small bar next to the gas station. Men stared as we sat down. My hair was a little long, hers a little short, both fine for our world of universities. I wanted coke but seeing nothing but beer on the bar, asked for one. Comments on my hair, the way I was dressed. I tried to look bored, common, local, as I watched in the mirror the loudest baiter. He didn't like my hair, laughed at my baggy khaki pants. My beer foamed as I squeezed the glass harder and harder. He was short, had long black hair, greased and combed straight back from his forehead. In his mocking he didn't notice dropping a 20 dollar bill as he bought beer for himself and his friends. The bill fell by my foot and I stepped on it. I stood at the bar that way a long time till he'd forgotten about me. I picked up the bill and brought it over to him. He checked his wallet and said a few feeble thank yous. He bought us beers and cokes until our car was fixed and said, "Good trip," as we left.

Only by accident will you ever be accepted as a brother if you are at all different. "The Answerer" shouldn't be the only choice. Whitman is obviously an answerer—able to be all humanity, but none particularly well.

Whitman seems out of touch with what's really possible and what he'd like to be possible. Man has to be afraid when he kisses man on a street corner. Black afraid when he walks through white. Long-haired seventh graders are sent home by the principal, men defending other's civil rights are killed and beaten, the sane are called the sick.

"To compare Whitman's poetry with other poetry is like comparing *Alice* to other books." A quip from Jarrell, but very much to the point. There is something here that's completely out of the realm of most poetry.

It's too easy to say—that's because it's not poetry, but songs and catalogues of poems, bits of things which are poems in themselves. The poetry of Whitman turns things to poems, frogs to princes with its power. It presents the objects in new form, explores rare aspects of situations. He may say that real things are the only real poems, and his poems just words, but it's not true. That is, his poems allow us to see things as poems we never would otherwise. It is completely different: (1) It's completely personal poetry. He exposes himself like no other man has in written form. He has put it all down without fear, every line full of nerve, like a slap in the face. (2) There are no answers in his poems, just questions. Re-evaluating the role of a poet to figure it all out, Whitman searches hard to find all the possibilities, then simply presents them to us to draw our own conclusions.

Anyone can read Whitman and find himself among the pages and find his own particular life celebrated. It is simply by listing everything that Whitman hopes readers will learn their faults as well as their joys. He hopes for a revolution as others read and learn how to understand others.

* * *

In "Children of Adam," Whitman pleads for a vision of love which is gradually becoming impossible. He praises the parts of the body, the functions of the body, as the most simple beauty possible. Nothing between men and women could be unpleasant. He praises the very odor, actions, juices, flesh, feel of physical love. He holds the answer for an American society on the verge of ruining simple beauty. Women today, with make-up, clothes, and underclothes, have such power to make themselves visions and images of beauty and sex. They can make themselves so beautiful to look at that artifice becomes much better than the real thing. To masturbate, thinking of that beautiful creature, becomes more satisfying than actually taking her to bed. Once this starts, lovemaking becomes a chore—an unpleasant thing. It's fun taking off the layers, but then she is naked—the false eyelashes fall off—the hairpiece becomes unattached and you are left with a normal pretty girl. Now she is nothing, you barely have energy or desire to sleep with her, you do to save face (she isn't what you want to make love to anymore . . .).

The actual biology of love that Whitman praises, that once was the whispered tabu of love bores you. The heavy smell, the wetness everywhere, the sounds, it hits you as primitive, crude, you get squeamish, cold. You think of her posed at the party, her backless, short, black-lace dress, her long stockinged legs, somehow that's what you want in bed, smiles, lace, flirting, perfume, a band playing Beatles.

Mass pressure from TV, radio, magazines, stores, is forcing men to abandon any image of simple beauty, return to inhibitions, abhor frantic passions, and forcing women to reject their born beauty, and search for it in boxes and tubes.

I had no answer, I was beginning to succumb to the world of fashion.

Whitman has the answer. After reading him there can be no question which is more beautiful, the blue lace demi-bra or the bare breast.

* * *

The wind has been trying the window all night and has fairly blown it open.

The rain has stopped. The damp cold wind blows through this stuffy room, tempting me with new air and I have been silly to stay indoors all night.

The professor talks and says good things compared to most.

He gives Whitman a chance and reads it over and over himself.

Whitman's voice becomes his voice.

The big window is wide open, not even a screen to separate me from the first days of spring.

He doesn't mind that we don't listen but stare out the window

following the grand sports car up the road

picking out a soft spot on the grass

imagining we could dive headlong through the window

landing softly in all that out of focus freshness.

* * *

Whitman helps each one of us get out of a rut. It's only possible because his poetry isn't afraid to be common lots of the time, mystic and bizarre the rest.

When you sit in a stream and watch for an hour the way water courses over a rock or look at a horizon, or a field, and the things hit you as much more than a rock, a horizon, a field, or on a hot summersday when you focus on the air two feet before your face, and swear you see little bits of color, sparkle, and dust moving, making up the air, or when you want to see what's over the next hill, you are reading Whitman.

Before Whitman, if something dropped into the toilet bowl, like the soap, or toothbrush, whatever, I'd fish for it with a hanger. Now, I'd roll up my sleeve and reach in.

Index

Index

Index

With Respect to Readers

Designed by R. E. Rosenbaum.
Composed by Vail-Ballou Press, Inc.,
in 11 point linotype Janson, 3 points leaded,
with display lines in Palatino.
Printed from type by Vail-Ballou Press, Inc.,
on Warren's No. 66 Text, 60 pound basis,
with the Cornell University Press watermark.
Bound by Vail-Ballou Press, Inc.,
in Interlaken Arco Linen (Group B)
and stamped in All Purpose imitation white gold.

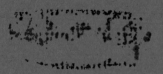